MW00366204

Are We There Yet?
DALLAS

A GUIDE TO FAMILY TRAVEL & ACTIVITIES

Written by Georgette Driscoll
Illustrated by Doris Kidby

Little Green Apples
TRAVEL GUIDES

Published by
LITTLE GREEN APPLES
TRAVEL GUIDES
Athens, Georgia

littlegreenapples.org

Text copyright © 2015 by Georgette Driscoll

Illustrations © 2015 Doris Kidby

Photographs © 2015 by John Driscoll

Text, book, and design by Georgette Driscoll

Original Artwork by Doris Kidby

Cover Photos & Editorial Assistance by John R. Driscoll

The author and publisher have made every effort to ensure the accuracy of the information in this book at the time of going to press. However, the publishers cannot accept any responsibility for any loss, injury, or inconvenience resulting from the use of information contained in this guide.

First Edition

ISBN# 978-0-9969730-0-7

Every effort has been made by the author and editors to make this guide as helpful and accurate as possible. Please keep in mind many things can change after publishing – new, wonderful attractions open or an establishment can close, move, restructure pricing, or hours of operation. Due to unforeseen changes, it is always best to call before an outing to confirm the details in this guide.

We appreciate any feedback and suggestions for future updates. Although we may not be able to respond to all comments and suggestions, we will take them to heart and share with the author.

Please send your suggestions to:

Little Green Apples Travel Guides

little.greenapples@outlook.com

Are We There Yet? Dallas

This book is dedicated to

My creative Mom

> *Thank you for your artistic view on life (and all the artwork in this book).*

My fantastic sisters, Angie and Donna

> *Thank you so much for exploring Dallas with us.*

My super kids, Jack and Walt

> *Have lots of adventures!*

My amazing husband, John

> *I love you more and more everyday.*

The memories we created in Dallas are everlasting. Thank you so much for being who you are and for encouraging me to always pursue my dreams.

Love,

Georgette

Are We There Yet? Dallas

Table of Contents

Introduction 1

   Traveling with Children 3

Texas and the Big D 7

   Texas is BIG 8

   Official State Symbols and Facts 9

   State Insects and Animals 10

   State Plants, Vegetables, and Food 10

   Texas Timeline 11

   Random Texas Facts 15

   Dallas is BIG too! 18

   Official City Symbols and Facts 19

   Brief History of Dallas 20

   Dallas Timeline 22

   Random Dallas Facts 24

The Best of BIG D 27

   It's really FREE! 29

   It's a really good deal! 31

   My Favorite Day! 33

   My Favorite Season: Spring! 37

   My Favorite Season: Summer! 41

   My Favorite Season: Fall! 43

   My Favorite Season: Winter! 49

   Best by Age 51

   The BEST Birthday Party! 55

   The BEST Sleepover 59

   The BEST Food 61

   The BEST Volunteer Experience 67

Art & Museums 71

Introduction 72

African American Museum 74

The Ann and Gabriel Barbier-Mueller Museum:
The Samurai Collection 75

Bath House Cultural Center 76

Crow Collection of Asian Art 77

Dallas Contemporary 78

Dallas Heritage Village at Old City Park 79

Dallas Holocaust Museum Center for Education and Tolerance ... 80

Dallas Museum of Art 81

Geometric MADI Museum 82

Goss-Michael Foundation 83

Heritage Farmstead Museum 84

International Museum of Cultures 86

Irving Arts Center 87

Latino Cultural Center 88

Meadows Museum of Art 90

Nasher Sculpture Center 91

National Scouting Museum 92

Oak Cliff Cultural Center 93

Old Red Museum
of Dallas County History & Culture 94

Perot Museum of Nature and Science 95

Perot Museum of Nature and Science at Fair Park 97

Sixth Floor Museum at Dealey Plaza 98

South Dallas Cultural Center 100

Texas Sculpture Garden 101

Film, Theatre, and the Sound of Music....................103

The Black Academy of Arts and Letters (TBAAL).....................104

Cara Mia Theater Company...................104

Children's Chorus of Greater Dallas...................105

Dallas Angelika Film Center: Crybaby Matinée...................105

Dallas Black Dance Theatre...................106

Dallas Children's Theater...................106

The Dallas Opera...................107

Dallas Puppet Theater...................107

Dallas Summer Musicals (DSM)...................108

Dallas Symphony Orchestra (DSO)...................109

Dallas Winds...................110

Fine Arts Chamber Players (FACP)...................110

Galaxy Drive-In...................111

Kathy Burks Theatre of Puppetry Arts...................111

Majestic Theatre...................112

Metropolitan Winds...................112

Meadows School of the Arts...................113

Morton H. Meyerson Symphony Center...................113

Music Hall at Fair Park...................114

Shakespeare Dallas...................114

Pocket Sandwich Theatre...................115

Texas Ballet...................115

Animals All Around...................117

The Children's Aquarium at Fair Park...................118

Dallas World Aquarium (DWA)...................120

Dallas Zoo...................122

The Gentle Zoo...................124

Heard Natural Science Museum and Wildlife Sanctuary...................125

Sea Life Grapevine Aquarium...................126

Texas Discovery Gardens in Fair Park...................127

Take it Outside (Parks and Recreation)

Take it Outside (Parks and Recreation) **129**

Abbott Park 130

Addison Circle Park 130

Bachman Lake / Bachman Lake Trail 131

Beckert Park 131

Bob Jones Nature Center and Preserve 132

Bob Woodruff Park 133

Campion Trails 133

Cedar Hill State Park & Joe Pool Lake 134

Cedar Ridge Preserve 134

Celebration Park 135

Celestial Park 135

Connemara Meadow Preserve 136

Dallas Arboretum and Botanical Gardens 137

Dragon Park 138

Duck Creek Greenbelt 138

Elm Fork Nature Preserve 139

Fair Park 140

Grapevine Springs Preserve 142

Joe Pool Lake 142

Joppa Preserve 143

Katy Trail 143

Kidd Springs Park 144

Kiest Park 144

Klyde Warren Park 145

Lake Cliff Park 146

Lakeside Park 146

Liberty Park 147

Lewisville Lake Environmental Learning Area (LLELA) 147

Main Street Garden Park 148

Moore Park 148

Oak Point Park & Nature Preserve 149

Plano Trails 149

Pleasant Oaks Park 150

Quorum Park 150

Reverchon Park 151

Robert E. Lee Park 152

Rowlett Creek Nature Preserve Trails 152

Trinity Forest and River 153

Trinity River Audubon Center 154

Trinity River Expeditions 156

Turtle Creek Greenbelt 156

White Rock Creek Trail 157

White Rock Lake 157

Take Me Out to the Ballgame **159**

Dallas Cowboys (NFL) 160

Dallas Desperados 162

Dallas Mavericks Basketball Club (NBA) 163

Dallas Polo Club 164

Dallas Stars Hockey Club (NHL) 165

Devil's Bowl Speedway 166

FC Dallas Soccer Club (MLS) 167

Frisco Rough Riders (MiLB) 168

Grand Prairie Airhogs 168

Lone Star Park 169

Mesquite Championship Rodeo 169

Texas Rangers 170

Trains, Planes, and Automobiles **173**

    Academy of Model Aeronautics 174

    Dallas Area Kitefliers Organization (DAKO) 174

    Dallas Firefighter's Museum 175

    Dallas Zoo / Monorail Safari 176

    Founders' Plaza Plane Observation Area 176

    Frisco Fire Safety Town 177

    Frontiers of Flight Museum 178

    Grapevine Vintage Railroad 179

    McKinney Avenue Trolley (M-Line) 180

    Museum of the American Railroad 180

The Traditional Fun Zones **181**

    Adventure Landing 182

    Amazing Jake's Food and Fun 182

    Bahama Beach Waterpark 183

    Bounce U 183

    Celebration Station 184

    Cosmic Jump Trampoline Entertainment Center 184

    Fort Paintball 185

    Hawaiian Falls Adventure Park 185

    Indoor Safari Park 186

    Lil Ninjas 186

    Lunar Mini Golf 187

    Main Event 187

    Pole Position Raceway 188

    Pump It Up 188

    Sandy Lake Amusement Park 189

    Six Flags Hurricane Harbor 190

    Six Flags Over Texas 190

    Skyline Trapeze 191

Speed Zone 191

Surf and Swim 192

Top Golf 192

Trinity Forest Aerial Adventure Park 193

Whirlyball and Laser Whirld 193

Zero Gravity Thrill Amusement Park Dallas 194

The Expected to the Unexpected 195

Dallas Public Libraries 196

Legoland Discovery Center 197

Medieval Times Dinner & Tournament 198

Palace of Wax, Ripley's Believe It or Not!
And Enchanted Mirror Maze 198

Reunion Tower 199

Room Escape Adventures 200

Southfork Ranch 201

St. Mark's School of Texas Planetarium and Observatory 201

Thanks-Giving Square 202

University of North Texas (UNT) Sky Theater 202

Historic Districts and Landmarks 203

Day Tripper 211

Fort Worth 213

Amon Carter Museum of American Art 214

Cloud 9 Living 214

Forest Park Railroad 215

Fort Worth Botanic Garden 215

Fort Worth Museum of Science and History 216

Fort Worth Nature Center & Refuge 217

Fort Worth Stockyards 218

Fort Worth Water Gardens 219

Kimbell Art Museum 220

The Modern 221

National Cowgirl Museum and Hall of Fame 222
National Multicultural Western Heritage Museum 222
Glen Rose 223
Dinosaur Valley State Park 224
Dinosaur World 225
Fossil Rim Wildlife Center 226
Tyler 227
Brookshire's World of Wildlife Museum & Country Store 228
Caldwell Zoo 228
Center for Earth and Space Science Education 229
Cherokee Trace Drive-Thru Safari 229
Discovery Science Place 230
East Texas Symphony Orchestra (ETSO) 230
Goodman-Legrand Museum and Garden 231
Tiger Creek Wildlife Refuge 231
Resources **233**
Important Numbers 233
Visitors Information 233
Discounts 234
Transportation 235
Publications 236
Additional Online Resources & Blogs 237
Index **239**

Introduction

One of the best pieces of advice I received as a new mother was from my sister-in-law Mary. She told me to take our kids everywhere, let them get out in the world, and even skip school when a day trip or vacation warrants it.

Even my wonderful friends who work in the most important profession in the world – teaching – agree that a day at the museum can be just as, or even more, beneficial than a day in the classroom. Now, don't go too wild…if your children are at the age where a day of missed school will result in a backlog of homework, really evaluate the consequences. But keep in mind that hands-on, up-close, and in-person experiences will encourage curiosity and help forge new connections.

Children are naturally inquisitive and being out in the world experiencing new places and activities fuels the desire to learn more. Imagine how many times you heard "What's that?" from your child. Now, imagine being asked this same question while walking through a museum or a garden. It can be fun to be stumped by a two year old. Joining them on the journey helps inspire a life-long pursuit of knowledge, an appreciation of diversity, and enjoyment for all the surprises the world has to offer. Exploring and learning together creates excitement and lasting memories that can't be traded for anything.

This book is devoted to parents who love to learn with their children. Although my "research" has been geared towards the age of my boys (five and four), I've worked hard to include opportunities for all ages. Be sure to spend some time reviewing the "Best of Dallas" chapter that includes suggestions by age, price, season, and even volunteer opportunities.

The "Texas and the Big D" chapter includes a brief history of Texas and Dallas which will provide you with some interesting background as you explore.

My friendship with Jennie Hansen encouraged plenty of random facts throughout the book. Additional inspiration for this book was provided by Silas and Katy Cunningham, two of the smartest kids I've ever met. Their inquisitive minds inspired the "Smarty Pants" sections in gray that deliver interesting tid-bits about Dallas and some of the things you and your children will see and experience.

Jeff Thurmond, Pearl Miner, Gena Hinson, Sara Didier, John Bowling, and Arnold Alvarez provided friendship, laughter, suggestions, and encouragement. I feel incredibly lucky to have made such wonderful friends in such a big city.

I'd also like to thank Jeff Fedro for bringing our family to Dallas and Rachel Austin, who encourages everyone she meets to pursue their dreams. Whenever I started to have doubt about writing this book, I would hear Rachel say "one chapter at a time" and get my second wind.

Last but not least, I must thank two of the kindest people I have ever met. Rebecca and Harvey Jenkins truly made our transition to Dallas welcoming. They're everlasting passion for knowledge and exploration is truly outstanding. I can't put into words how grateful it is to have them as part of our extended family.

Enough of this mushy stuff - Now, get out there and explore Dallas!

Traveling with Children

The following are suggestions to help make your family travel experiences as smooth and rewarding as possible.

Go with the flow: You may or may not be a planner, but if you are - try to ease up a bit. Take some reality checks on what you and your family will want to do and can accomplish together. Don't create pressure to see and do everything. If a particular part of the museum delights your children, linger and enjoy it rather than rushing to the next exhibit.

We all need a little quiet time: Mom, dad, relatives, friends and even the kids can use a little break from jam packed activities. Arrange for some quiet and peaceful moments. Green spaces can be perfect for this. Taking time for a picnic or a simple walk through the park can be even more rewarding than heading to the next tourist destination.

The youngest one wins: When planning a trip, keep the youngest child in mind. Their safety and comfort can make or break a trip for the entire family. That said, invite all the children in the family to decide on possible options that everyone will enjoy. Providing your children with the opportunity to provide suggestions and make decisions empowers them and helps creates self-esteem.

Weekday fun: Weekday exploration is fantastic with shorter lines and less crowded venues. There are also great offers that only apply during the week. I work full time "plus" at my day job, but plan one vacation day per month so we can take advantage of the weekday offers. By keeping this a priority on our hectic calendar, I gain more work / life balance and the entire family benefits from the special time we get together.

Talk about it: After the museum visit, ask your kids what their favorite painting was and why. After the zoo, talk about the different habitats and what the zoo keeper must do to take care of the animals. Talk about the colors, shapes, and noises. Talk, talk, talk...but don't forget to listen. Asking your children's opinion and actively listening shows you value them.

Be present: It saddens me how many times I see parents glued to their iPhone while their children struggle for attention. It will come too soon – before you know it your kids will be moving out or heading to college. You will never have another today to spend with your kids, so make the most of every opportunity.

Local Explorers

Dallas is the perfect place to take a "stay-vacation". There is so much to offer and enjoy in this big city.

When traveling locally, think about the essentials and don't weigh yourself down with every possible thing in the diaper bag. This prospect may sound scary, but consider leaving the stroller behind and using a baby sling or toddler back pack instead. You'll be able to get around a lot easier and the view will often be more rewarding for your little ones.

You may want to consider having a dedicated travel bag ready to go. Some suggestions for your travel bag:

- Bottled Water

- Light snacks, such as granola bars or crackers

- A lightweight distractor, such as a sticker book

- Sunscreen

- Bug Spray

- Antibiotic ointment and a few bandages

- A few diapers and a change of clothes

Remember, you're trying to lighten the load so don't over do it.

Up in the Air

A child's first flight can be thrilling and daunting. Start preparations early so you can reserve the seats you want and understand the regulations for luggage, carry on, bottles, and child seats.

You should also start mentally preparing your child for the adventure by reading airport and airplane books. Talk about what to expect, like the security gates and the bumps and sounds they will hear during take-off, in flight, and during the landing.

Pack your carry on accordingly with lots of small quiet activities to keep them preoccupied on a long flight.

On the Road

Think about what type of travel time works best for your family. Some prefer to hit the road early or very late allowing the kids to sleep through part of the trip. Regardless of what time you set out, expect and be prepared to make lots of stops.

With this in mind, do some research before a long trip to see if there are some interesting historic diners, parks, or attractions along the way. Again – be flexible.

I once had my mind set on having a picnic at a great national park that was about three hours into the road trip. With the park still an hour away, the crankies set in. I was so glad that I took the next exit and found a perfect little city park instead of pushing on to my planned destination. Being flexible saved the trip.

What to bring...

It's hard, but don't pack the entire house into the mini-van. Think about what you'll really need. Some suggestions:

- Travel bag (see suggestions on the previous page)

- Emergency medical kit:
  - Aspirin or an aspirin substitute
  - Cough syrup and decongestant
  - Medication to relieve diarrhea
  - Antibiotic ointment and a few bandages
  - Ointments to soothe sunburn, rashes, and poison ivy
  - Any medications taken on a regular basis or needed in case of emergencies

- Snack and drink bags:
  - Pack your families favorite healthy and portable foods, like apples, bananas, oranges, snack crackers, etc.
  - Bring lots of bottled water
  - A cooler with fruit juices, string cheese, and pre-made sandwiches
  - Extra bottles and sippy cups as well as liquid detergent and a sponge

- Travel toys and books: Consider a special activity travel bag with coloring books and crayons, quiet toys, and sticker books. Include small and easy to grab items that encourage your kids to burn off excess energy when at a stop. Think jump ropes, a small football, and sidewalk chalk.

- Stop Watch: Yes, a stop watch. It's small and can be used in all kinds of ways along the road. Use it with all the verbal trivia games you'll come up with, a timer to encourage extra races at the rest stop, etc.

- Clothing (with extra layers and changes)

- Extra shoes

- Extra empty tote bags – you'll end up using them for something (dirty laundry, sippy cups, etc.)

- If you have a long road trip with a hotel stay planned along the way, pack one bag with just the items for that night. You won't have to tote in all the luggage!

- A small gift for your hosts if staying with friends or relatives.

Are We There Yet?

You will hear it multiple times....

Here's a fun way to provide a visual answer.

Put a long piece of Velcro along the interior of your vehicle.

Mark off significant destination points that you will reach along the way.

On a small toy car, place another piece of Velcro.

Ask your kids to move the car along as your trip progresses.

Over achievers: For each destination mark, have a new activity planned.

Texas and the Big D

Texas is BIG

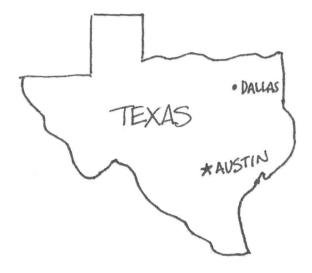

Size:

Texas is the second largest state in the US with 268,820 square miles. There are more than 70,000 miles of highway in Texas with more than a million signs and markers.

Population:

After California, Texas is the second most populous state in the U.S. with a reported population of 25,145,561 (2010 U.S. Census report).

This is a population density of 96.3 people per square mile.

How much paint would it take to put stripes along all of the highways in Texas?

1.6 million gallons of white and yellow paint!

Official State Symbols and Facts

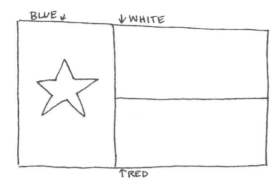

The colors on the flag symbolize:
Red: bravery
White: purity and liberty
Blue: loyalty

Texas is the only state to have the flags of six different nations fly over it (Spain, France, Mexico, Republic of Texas, Confederate States, and the United States).

The nickname "Lone Star State" is based on the one star on the Texas flag and represents the struggles for independence from Mexico.

The state seal is one star, an oak branch (strength) and an olive branch (peace).

The state motto is "friendship".

The name Texas came from the Caddoan Native American tribe who greeted friends by saying "tejas".

The official state song, "Texas, Our Texas", was written by composer William J. Marsh and lyricist Gladys Yoakum Wright. Texas's official dance is the square dance. The subject of the song "The Yellow Rose of Texas" was Emily Morgan, an African American indentured servant.

The state sport is rodeo.

State Insects and Animals

State Bird: Mockingbird

State Insect: Monarch butterfly

State Fish: Guadalupe bass

State Large Mammal: Longhorn bull

State Small Mammal: Armor-plated armadillo

State Flying Mammal: Mexican free-tailed bat

State Fish: Guadalupe bass

Butterflies and Armadillos

The monarch butterfly is the only butterfly species that does not hibernate. It migrates to Mexico in the changing seasons.

Armadillos always have four babies. They have one egg, which splits into four, and they either have four males or four females.

State Plants, Vegetables, and Food

The state flower of Texas is the bluebonnet, also known as "buffalo clovers" and "wolf flowers". This beautiful flower can be found growing wild in the country. In addition to the bluebonnet, more than 4,000 different kinds of wildflowers grow in Texas.

Texas was the first state to choose a state tree - the pecan tree. Some native pecan trees are estimated to be 150 years old and can grow an average of 70-100 feet tall.

The state champion pecan is located in Franklin County. It is 111 inches in circumference, 115 feet tall, and has a crown spread of 66 feet.

State Grass: Sideoats Grama

State Pepper : Jalapeño

State Vegetable: 1015 sweet onion

State Fruit: Texas red grapefruit

The official dish of Texas is chili.

Texas Timeline

Some anthropologists estimate primitive people existed in Texas as far back as 37,000 years ago. Lubbock Lake Park continues to reveal a history of 12,000 years of occupation by ancient people of the Southern High Plains and an equally ancient burial site was discovered at Permian Basin in West Texas.

Between 12,000 to 8,000 years ago, small bands of nomadic hunters lived in Texas. The Folsom, Clovis, and Plainview cultures shared many hunting techniques, such as making weapons from chipped stone and knives from flint. Based on the season, the people moved to where the plants and animals would provide valuable resources.

East Texas provided fertile soil and plenty or rainfall making it easy to plant crops. The coastal areas of Texas provided small game and food from the Gulf. Buffalo, elk, and deer roamed North, West, and Central Texas. The people in the North Central areas of Texas combined many of the lifestyles of their neighbors.

By the time the Europeans arrived the frontier was complex with Comanche, Caddo, Apache, Karankawa, Tonkawa, Wichita, and many other tribes living throughout Texas.

There are three reservations in Texas.

Alabama-Coushatta Tribe of Texas
Rt 3 Box 640
Livingston, TX 77351

Kickapoo Traditional Tribe of Texas
HC1 Box 9700
Eagle Pass, TX 78852

Ysleta del Sur Pueblo
PO Box 17579, Ysleta Stn
El Paso, TX 79917

1519	Multiple Native Americans are living in area; Alonso Alvarez de Pineda of Spain sails into Rio Grande and maps the Texas coast.
1681	Ysleta, the oldest European settlement in Texas, is established by Spanish Franciscan missionaries.
1718	The mission that is now known as the Alamo is founded.
1772	San Antonio is named the center of Spanish government in Texas.
1819	Several hundred Cherokees move to Texas to flee pressures from settlers to the north and east.
1821	Texas becomes a state within the republic of Mexico.
1830	The Kickapoos arrive in Texas after being crowded out by settlers in the Great Lakes area.
1836	Texans gained independence from Mexico and the Republic of Texas is declared. During 1836, five sites served as temporary capitals.
1837	Sam Houston moved the capital to Houston.
1839	The capital was moved to Austin.
1845	Texas became the 28th state in the U.S. and was admitted into the Union on December 29, 1845. Texas entered the United States by treaty whereas all other states entered by territorial annexation.
1846	Mexican War begins in Texas.

There have been eight changes of government

Spanish 1519-1685	Mexican 1821-1836	Confederate States 1861-1865
French 1685-1690	Republic of Texas 1836-1845	United States 1865-present
Spanish 1690-1821	United States 1845-1861	

1861 Texas secedes from the Union and joins the Confederacy in Civil War.

1870 Texas is readmitted to the Union.

1870s The Mescalero Apaches left for Mexico and New Mexico reservations.

1875 The military forced the last Native Americans living east of the Pecos River into the Oklahoma territory.

1883 The University of Texas opens in Austin.

1888 The capital building in Austin opens.

1900 The worst natural disaster in the United States is a hurricane that strikes Galveston killing eight thousand people.

1901 Oil boom begins with a discovery at Spindletop Hill near Beaumont.

1919 Texas approves women's right to vote.

1961 The Manned Spacecraft Center in Houston is opened by the National Aeronautics and Space Administration (NASA).

1963 Texan Lyndon B. Johnson becomes the 36th president after President John F. Kennedy is assassinated in Dallas on November 22, 1963.

1972 Houston-born Barbara Jordan becomes the first black southern woman to be elected to the U.S. House of Representatives.

1980s An explosion of filming arrives in Texas, including *Raggedy Man, Dallas, The Best Little Whorehouse in Texas,* and *All the Pretty Horses.*

1993 Branch Davidians standoff with federal law-enforcement near Waco.

1995 New Mission Control facility opens in July at the Johnson Space Center in Houston.

2003 Space Shuttle Columbia disintegrates over Texas and Louisiana as it reentered Earth's atmosphere. All seven crew members died.

2005 Hurricane Rita made landfall between Texas and Louisiana on September 24th. Rita was the fourth most intense Atlantic hurricane and the most intense tropical cyclone ever recorded.

2012 Record outbreak of the West Nile Virus in North Texas creates a state of emergency.

Random Texas Facts

I remember hearing this story on "The Rest of the Story" with Paul Harvey when I was a kid and I always loved it. Charles Alderton worked at a drug store and wanted to date the daughter of a local doctor. To impress the father and win the heart of the daughter, he invented a new drink in 1885...Dr Pepper. He didn't win over the father or the daughter, but Dr Pepper is still in existence today. Be sure to make a stop at the Dublin Bottling Works which has been bottling sodas in Dublin, Texas for more than 120 years.

 Texas wins the prize for most tornadoes per year with an average of 139 per year. Texas also holds the US 24 hour rainfall record with an amazing 43 inches splashing down on Alvin during the 1979 Topical Storm Claudette.

The oldest tree in the state is a coastal live oak located near Fulton - estimated age is more than 1,500 years old.

The Dallas/Fort Worth International Airport (DFW) wins the prize for the world's largest parking lot.

The city of Slaughter, Texas, has never had a homicide.

"Calf fries" are bull testicles that are greased, battered, and deep fried. Both Vinita, Oklahoma and Amarillo, Texas claim to have the "World's Largest Calf Fry Cook Off".

I'll let you decide....

Are there any natural lakes in Texas?

Only one - Caddo Lake in Karnack, Texas.

As the first governor of Texas, Sam Houston, is one of the most famous Texans, but he was actually born in Virginia. Being that he also served as governor of Tennessee, he is the only person to become governor of two different US states through popular election. If you find yourself on Interstate 45 near Huntsville, Texas, be sure to check out the statue of Sam Houston called a "Tribute to Courage".

Often attributed to Sam Houston is the famous battle cry "Remember the Alamo!", but it was actually coined by Sidney Sherman, a Texas General during the Texas Revolution.

Jim "Pa" Ferguson, Texas Governor from 1915 – 1917, was impeached for misapplication of public funds. A few years later, his wife Miriam Amanda Wallace "Ma" Ferguson ran under the slogan "two governors for the price of one" vowing to allow Jim to govern over her shoulder. In 1925, "Ma" became the first woman elected governor of Texas.

The first word spoken from the moon was "Houston" on July 20, 1969.

There are more species of bats in Texas than anywhere else in the United States.

US Presidents born in Texas:

Dwight D. Eisenhower and Lyndon B. Johnson

US Presidents that died in Texas:

John F. Kennedy was assassinated in Dallas on November 22, 1963.

Lyndon B. Johnson died at the same place he was born, the Johnson ranch outside Stonewall. He suffered a fatal coronary on January 22, 1973.

Lyndon B. Johnson taught at a high school in Houston before becoming President.

Are We There Yet? Dallas

The 22 acre Tyler Municipal Rose Garden is home to 38,000 rose bushes, making it the worlds' largest rose garden.

Texas can claim the first rodeo which was held in Pecos on July 4, 1883.

Some Famous Texans:

Alvin Ailey	Dancer
Stephen F. Austin	First Secretary of State
Gail Borden	Inventor of canned milk
Carol Burnett	Comedian and actress
Van Cliburn	Pianist
Joan Crawford	Actress
Dwight D. Eisenhower	Military leader and US President
Horton Foote	Author and playwright
Buddy Holly	Musician
Howard Robert Hughes	Industrialist, aviator, producer
John Arthur "Jack" Johnson	Boxer
Lyndon Baines Johnson	US President
Scott Joplin	Musician
Barbara Jordan	Senator
Larry McMurty	Author
Willie Nelson	Musician
H. Ross Perot	Businessman
Sandra Day O'Connor	Supreme Court Justice

The Heisman trophy is named after John William Heisman who was an athletic director at Rice University in Houston.

Texas towns with unusual names: Trickham (originally Trick 'Em); Happy; Oatmeal; Gun Barrel City; Sundown; Panhandle; Sugar Land; Lone Star; Cactus; Earth; and Buffalo. There used to be a community called Ding Dong in Bell County.

Dallas is BIG too!

Size & Location:

Dallas is 385.8 square miles located in the Central Time Zone in
North Central Texas. It is 35 miles east of Fort Worth, 245 miles
northwest of Houston, and 300 miles north of the Gulf of Mexico.

The Dallas area is the largest metropolitan area in the nation not on a
navigable body of water.

Population & Visitors:

With a population of 1,241,000, Dallas is the 9th largest city in the US
and the third largest in Texas. The median age is 32 and 28% of the
population have a bachelor's degree or higher.

The Dallas-Fort Worth Arlington Metroplex is the No. 1 visitor and
leisure destination in Texas. Dallas alone has 22.6 million visitors per
year.

Between the two airports (Dallas/Ft. Worth International and Dallas
Love Field) more than 2,000 flights arrive daily. There are more than
30,000 hotel rooms in the city of Dallas.

Official City Symbols and Facts

Name Origin

This one is a little tricky as there is not a definite answer. Most believe Dallas was named after US Vice President, George Mifflin Dallas. However, there is no linkage between George Mifflin Dallas and John Neely Bryan, the founder of Dallas.

> *John Neely Bryan passed away in the State Lunatic Asylum in Austin in 1877.*

Nickname: The Big D

This nickname comes from the 1960s movie *The Big D* which was filmed at Fair Park.

City Slogan: Big Things Happen Here

Dallas is home to five professional sports teams: The Dallas Cowboys (NFL); Dallas Stars (NHL); Dallas Mavericks (NBA); FC Dallas (MLS); and the Texas Rangers (MLB).

Elevation: 450-750 feet

Temperature and Rainfall:

Average minimum temperature is 55 degrees Fahrenheit

Average maximum temperature is 76 degrees Fahrenheit

Dallas has an average annual rainfall of 33.3 inches (84.6 centimeters)

Brief History of Dallas

In 1839, John Neely Bryan was searching for the ideal location
for a trading post. After surveying the area that became Dallas,
he returned to his home in Arkansas to prepare his plans. When
he returned to the area in 1841, he found that a treaty removing
Native Americans from the area had been signed and most of his
prospective customers were gone.

He abandoned his trading post plan and created a permanent
settlement which was founded in November 1841. Dallas quickly
grew as a service town for the rural areas surrounding it. By 1850,
the city included a grocery store, drugstore, insurance agency, and
a factory manufacturing carriages. On February 2, 1856, Dallas was
granted a town charter.

In 1857, the nearby Utopian artist and musician society, La Reunion,
collapsed. Many of the 350 French, Belgian, and Swiss colonists
that made up the community were displaced into Dallas. Others
remained on the La Reunion land near the forks of the Trinity River.
In 1860, this area was also incorporated into Dallas.

Between 1860 and 1870, the Dallas population grew from 678 to
3,000. A large part of the growth was due to Dallas being a long way
from any actual battle during the Civil War and former Texas slaves
moving to Dallas as it was more prosperous than other southern
cities. The new growth spurred on railroad routes which started to
intersect Dallas. At the time, cotton was the areas principal crop and
Dallas became the world center for leather trade.

By 1880, the population had grown to 10,385. The professional sector
also emerged with banking and insurance firms. By 1890, Dallas was
the most populous city in Texas with 38,067 residents.

The national financial crisis in the early 1890s hit Dallas hard.
Several banks and factories failed. However, in the years to come the
city began to recover. The restored growth helped ignite workers.
The American Federation of Labor granted a charter to the Trades
Assembly of Dallas in 1899. Some of their earliest championships
included the eight hour work day and legislation outlawing the
firing of union members.

Business, industry, and the population continued to grow during
the turn of the century. By 1910, the population reached 92,104. The
opening of the Federal Reserve Bank in 1914 and a Ford assembly
plant helped the population almost double in the next ten years.

By 1930, the population had reached 260,475 and another 30,000 people moved to Dallas during the Great Depression. The East Texas discovery of oil in 1930 and a new financial market for oil reserve financing reduced some of the effects of the Great Depression in Dallas. Additional jobs were created in Dallas when Fair Park was chosen for the Texas Centennial celebration in 1936.

After World War II, Dallas experienced another large manufacturing boom period. By 1950, the population was 434,462. New growth in the 1950 and 1960s was mainly tied to the technological and wholesale trade.

Dallas of the 1960s is best known for the assassination of President John F. Kennedy on November 22, 1963. He was pronounced dead at the Parkland Memorial Hospital just a few blocks away from Dealey Plaza. Just over two hours after the assassination, Lyndon B. Johnson took the oath of office at Love Field on Air Force One. This tragic moment in American history defined Dallas for much of the country. With great care, the city has moved to embrace this significant moment in history and create opportunities to honor the legacy of the President.

The Dallas-Fort Worth International Airport was opened in 1973 and attracted multiple businesses which moved or opened their headquarters in the area. A technology boom in the 1990s continued this growth.

By the year 2010, the population rose to 2,368,139. That same year, the Dallas Independent School District became the eighth largest school district in the nation, with more than 130,000 students. The growth of the town also encouraged many higher learning educational institutions to open or relocate in Dallas. The large population of Dallas brought a wealth of cultural, sports, and outdoor options for both visitors and residents.

1841	Permanent settlement
1856	February 2, 1856: Granted town charter.
1888	Dallas Zoo opened with two mountain lions and two deer. It was the first zoological garden in the state. Dallas' first "skyscraper", the six-story North Texas Building, is erected.
1890	Texas State Fair and Dallas Exposition attracts nearly 35,000 visitors.
1905	Theodore Roosevelt gives speech at the Oriental Hotel. Thus marking the first presidential visit to Dallas.
1930	Oil strike in Kilgore (100 miles east of Dallas) spawned the East Texas oil boom and Dallas quickly became the financial center for the oil industry in Texas and Oklahoma.

Bonnie and Clyde met in a West Dallas neighborhood and began their crime spree across Texas, Oklahoma, and Louisiana. They were buried in Dallas after being killed by police in Louisiana on May 23, 1934. |
| 1936 | Texas Centennial Exposition with more than fifty buildings constructed in Fair Park. |

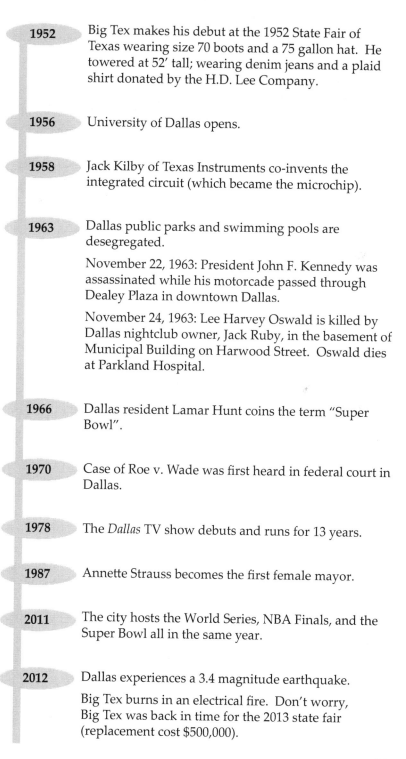

1952 Big Tex makes his debut at the 1952 State Fair of Texas wearing size 70 boots and a 75 gallon hat. He towered at 52' tall; wearing denim jeans and a plaid shirt donated by the H.D. Lee Company.

1956 University of Dallas opens.

1958 Jack Kilby of Texas Instruments co-invents the integrated circuit (which became the microchip).

1963 Dallas public parks and swimming pools are desegregated.

November 22, 1963: President John F. Kennedy was assassinated while his motorcade passed through Dealey Plaza in downtown Dallas.

November 24, 1963: Lee Harvey Oswald is killed by Dallas nightclub owner, Jack Ruby, in the basement of Municipal Building on Harwood Street. Oswald dies at Parkland Hospital.

1966 Dallas resident Lamar Hunt coins the term "Super Bowl".

1970 Case of Roe v. Wade was first heard in federal court in Dallas.

1978 The *Dallas* TV show debuts and runs for 13 years.

1987 Annette Strauss becomes the first female mayor.

2011 The city hosts the World Series, NBA Finals, and the Super Bowl all in the same year.

2012 Dallas experiences a 3.4 magnitude earthquake.

Big Tex burns in an electrical fire. Don't worry, Big Tex was back in time for the 2013 state fair (replacement cost $500,000).

23

Random Dallas Facts

The frozen margarita machine was invented in Dallas by Mariano Martinez in 1971. His first machine, inspired by a Slurpee machine, was inducted into the Smithsonian's National Museum of American History in Washington, D.C. in 2005. Enjoy one of those famous margaritas when you dine at Mariano's Mexican Cuisine (locations throughout Dallas).

Speaking of Slurpees, the nation's first Seven-Eleven opened in Oak Cliff in 1927.

Dallas is home to 18 Fortune 500 companies including JC Penny, Exxon Mobil, AT&T, and Texas Instruments.

Dallas ranks #3 on the best list of places for women to launch businesses.

Twenty-three of the richest Americans live in the The Dallas/Fort Worth Metroplex. So what do all those rich people do? They shop! In 1907, Herbert Marcus opened a Dallas store that grew into Neiman-Marcus. It's also very fitting that Highland Park Village Shopping Center, developed in 1931, has the distinction of being the first planned shopping center in America.

The entire Statue of Liberty could fit into the Cowboys Stadium.

The Dallas Cowboys were originally known as the Dallas Steers. The name was quickly changed when the team's manager decided he didn't want a castrated mascot. Dallas' earliest professional baseball team was called The Hams. Houston's first team had an equally timid name - The Babies.

In 1972, Dallas became home to the NFL's first ever professional cheer-leading squad.

There are over 168 listings for donut shops in Dallas.

Are We There Yet? Dallas

*Did you know German chocolate cake
has nothing to do with Germany?*

The recipe gained popularity after an
American, Sam German, published his
recipe in the Dallas Morning Star.

The Galleria Dallas is home to the tallest indoor Christmas tree.

Dallas Children's Medical Center displays the largest
permanent model train exhibit in the country.

The Dallas Arts District is the largest urban arts district in the United States. When completed, the Trinity River Corridor will be more than ten times the size of Central Park.

Barney, the lovable purple dinosaur, was "born" in Dallas.

Some of the movies/TV series filmed in the area: *Dallas*; *Silkwood*; *Places in the Heart*; *Prison Break*; *Born on the Fourth of July*; *Walker, Texas Ranger*; and *Robo Cop*.

The TV drama series *Dallas* ran from 1978 to 1991 and has been dubbed into 67 languages and broadcast in more than 90 countries. It was filmed on location at the Cloyce Box Ranch in Frisco, Texas, outside of Dallas. Definitely visit there!

"Who Done It?" the 1980 episode of *Dallas* that revealed who shot J.R. Ewing, had the largest international audience of any single television episode in history, with about 360 million viewers worldwide. So who done it? I know, but I won't say...watch it!

A few celebrities from the area: Angie Harmon; Luke and Owen Wilson; Nastia Luikin; Vanilla Ice; Meatloaf; Lee Trevino; Norah Jones; Erykah Badu; and Jessica Simpson.

Are We There Yet? Dallas

The Best of BIG D

Let me introduce you to the "coffee stain" chapter. Why call it that? Because this will probably be the chapter your reference the most. This chapter includes lists of the BEST by price (at least 50 of which are FREE), day of the week, season, age, birthday parties, sleepovers, and food. In addition, there is a great list of ways in which children of all ages can volunteer.

Since day of week specials and festival dates are likely to change, be sure to contact the attraction before making plans. Most of the attractions in the lists have a full description provided in the following chapters. If not, a web site has been provided with the list entry.

Are We There Yet? Dallas

It's Really FREE!

- Academy of Model Aeronautics (AMA): Membership is free for children 19 and younger. AMA also provides the opportunity to see demonstrations and competitions.

- African American Museum

- Amon Carter Museum of American Art (Fort Worth)

- Ann & Gabriel Barbier-Mueller Museum: The Samurai Collection

- Bath House Culture Center: Gallery is free

- Bob Jones Nature Center

- Cedar Ridge Preserve

- Crow Collection of Asian Art: Free admission and some classes.

- Dallas Area Kitefliers Organization: Check the website for fly dates and locations.

- Dallas Contemporary

- Dallas Heritage Village at Old City Park: Free admission for children on the first Sunday per month.

- Dallas Mavericks Basketball: Mavs Kids Club is free.

- Dallas Museum of Art

- The Dallas Opera: Free Dress Rehearsals and Opera Boot Camp

- Dallas Public Libraries: Do not miss out! Check the website for a wonderful variety of programs for kids and teens.

- Dallas Stars Hockey Club: Little Rookies, a hockey trial camp available at the Dr Pepper Star Centers, is free for first-time players.

- Dallas Summer Musicals: Join the DSM Kids Club for free and receive invitation to club events.

- Dallas Symphony Orchestra: Check the website as some community concerts are free to the public.

- FC Dallas Soccer Club (MLS): Participate in your local library's reading program for complimentary tickets.

- Fine Arts Chamber Players: Free classical concerts and educational programs.

- Frisco Fire Safety Town (Frisco): Learn about safety while walking through the a miniature version of Frisco.

It's Really FREE!

- Frisco Rough Riders: Join Deuce's Birthday club to receive a free ticket during the month of your child's birthday.
- Geometric MADI Museum
- Goss-Michael Foundation
- International Museum of Cultures: Offers free admission days. Check the website for the current opportunities.
- Klyde Warren Park: Family Experiment days brought to you by Perot Museum. Check the Perot Museum website for hands on investigation and experiment dates at the park.
- Latino Cultural Center
- McKinney Avenue Transit Authority (M-Line): Free rides on the fully restored vintage trolleys providing service in the Uptown neighborhood.
- Meadows Museum of Art: Free admission on Thursdays after 5pm.
- Medieval Times Dinner & Tournament: Free on your birthday.
- Metropolitan Winds: Check the website as some community concerts are free to the public.
- The Modern (Fort Worth): Free on Sundays / Half price on Wednesdays.
- Nasher Sculpture Center: Free the first Saturday per month from 10am – 5pm. Also look for free evening events and outdoor films.
- National Scouting Museum: Free admission on Sunday and Monday.
- Oak Cliff Cultural Center
- South Dallas Cultural Center
- St. Mark's School of Texas Planetarium and Observatory: Open to the public. Check the calendar of events for options.
- Texas Ballet: Check the website as some community performances are free to the public.
- Texas Discovery Gardens: Free admission to the gardens on Tuesdays (butterfly house is regular admission).
- Texas Sculpture Garden (Frisco)
- Trinity River Audubon Center: Free general admission on the third Thursday of each month. Also check the website in the summer as there have been special promotions in which access is free any day in the summer months.
- The Wilson House Tour: Provided by Preservation Dallas on Tuesdays through Friday from 10am to 4pm.

Are We There Yet? Dallas

It's a really good deal!

- Cedar Hill State Park: Feel like you have really left the city by visiting this excellent state park. Low park entry fees and great deals on boat, bike, and kayak rentals.

- Children's Aquarium at Fair Park: Very low admission cost and children 2 and under are free. Your family will want to go more than once, so take advantage of the annual pass price.

- Dallas Heritage Village

- The Dallas Opera: $4 student matinées.

- Dallas Zoo: Normal admission is at a pretty great price and gets even better in Jan. and Feb. when tickets are reduced to $5.

- FC Dallas Soccer Club (MLS): Games as low as $20. Participate in your local library's reading program for complimentary tickets.

- Forest Park Miniature Railroad (Fort Worth): Five mile miniature train ride that crosses six bridges with an adult ticket cost of $4.

- Fort Worth Botanic Gardens: Children under 4 are free. Adults $2 and kids 4-12 are only $1.

- Frontiers of Flight Museum: So much to offer for a low admission price. Great classes, camps, and birthday party opportunities as well.

- Heritage Farmstead Museum (Plano)

- Old Red Museum of Dallas County History & Culture: Early bird special on Sundays if tickets are purchased before noon.

- The Perot Museum Fair Park Campus: $1 will get you into the Nature Building at Fair Park .

- Sandy Lake Amusement Park: $2 admission and super inexpensive ride, golf, and pool tickets.

- Surf and Swim (Garland): Low cost water park. Save more money by bringing your own food – coolers are permitted, but no glass.

- Texas Discovery Gardens: Low admission cost with lots of activities and special events.

- Texas Rangers: Jr. Rangers Club Membership for $20 includes four ticket vouchers and many other goodies and perks. Available for children 13 and under.

- Trinity River Audubon Center: Low general admission fees and free general admission on the third Thursday of each month.

Are We There Yet? Dallas

My Favorite Day!

This list provides deals or special events by the day of the week. Please check the website or contact the attraction before making plans as these are subject to change. Contact and additional information about each attraction is provided in the following chapters.

Monday

- Dallas Zoo: Ride DART to the Zoo to get $2 off admission
- National Scouting Museum: Free admission

Tuesday

- The Ann and Gabriel Barbier-Muller Museum: The Samurai Collection: Stays open until 8pm
- Celebration Station: Unlimited Rides
- Dallas Angelika Film Center: Crybaby Matinée is available
- Dallas Museum of Art: First Tuesday series (1st Tuesday/month)
- Dallas Zoo: Ride DART to the Zoo to get $2 off admission
- Klyde Warren Park: Imagination Playground blocks are available at the park. Build a mini-Dallas in the heart of Dallas.
- Texas Discovery Gardens: Free admission to the gardens (butterfly house is regular admission)

Wednesday

- Celebration Station: Double Your Fun Wednesday Promotions
- Dallas Angelika Film Center: Crybaby Matinée is available
- Dallas Heritage Village: Nip and Tuck's Barnyard Buddy Stories on the second Wednesday per month
- Dallas Zoo: $5 Senior Admission
- The Modern (Fort Worth): Half Price
- Perot Museum: Story Time Under the Stars on the last Wednesday/month

My Favorite Day!

Thursday

- Celebration Station: Family Fun Day (unlimited outdoor rides and pizza buffet)
- Dallas Arboretum: Cool Thursday Concert Series on the lawn in Spring, Summer, and Fall
- Dallas Museum of Art: Stays open until 9pm
- Irving Arts Center: Stays open until 8pm
- Meadows Museum of Art: Free admission on Thursdays after 5pm
- Perot Museum: Stays open until 9pm. First Thursday/month provides an educational botanical program and the be sure to visit "The Lab" on the second Thursday/month
- Pocket Sandwich Theatre: Enjoy lower admission fee
- Trinity River Audubon Center: Free general admission on the third Thursday of each month

Friday

- Bounce U (Plano): Parent's Night Out every other Friday.
- Crow Collection of Asian Art: On the third Fridays of March, June, and September enjoy the Crow Collection After Dark. Each free themed event includes music, dance, films, and tours.
- Dallas Museum of Art: Late Nights on the third Friday/month
- Dallas Zoo: Check online for the Safari Nights hike schedule
- Heritage Farmstead Museum: Fun on the Farm Fridays
- Lewisville Lake Environmental Learning Area: Primitive camping available on Friday and Saturday nights

Saturday

- Bob Jones Nature Center: Camera Club

- Cedar Ridge Preserve: The third Saturday per month is Habitat Restoration and Trail Maintenance time. Tools, snacks, and water are provided. Contact info_CRP@yahoo.com for more information.

- Crow Collection of Asian Art: Yoginos is available every Saturday; Young Dragons and Adventure Asia on the first Saturday/month and Studio Saturdays on the second Saturday/month.

- Dallas Zoo: Check online for the Safari Nights hike schedule

- Devil's Bowl Speedway: Dirt Track Racing every Saturday from mid-March through October

- Goss – Michael Foundation: Saturday Sketch days on select Saturdays

- Grapevine Vintage Railroad: Saturday Morning Fun Trains

- Heard Natural Science Museum and Wildlife Sanctuary: Third Saturday Nature Talks

- Latino Cultural Center: Target Second Saturday provides a unique experience with dance, theater, and workshops (2nd Saturday/month).

- Lewisville Lake Environmental Learning Area: Third Saturday of each month tour the Minor-Porter Log Home or kayak Elm Fork with the experts at Kayakpower.com. Primitive camping available on Friday and Saturday nights.

- Nasher Sculpture Center: Free on the first Saturday/month

- Perot Museum: Discovery Days on the second Saturday/month

- Trinity River Audubon Center: Get the kids connected to the community on the 2nd Saturday per month from 9am – 12pm. 11 years and older can volunteer with Habitat Restoration Day.

- Trinity River Expeditions: Guided tours available the second Saturday per month, with a change in location every month.

- UNT Sky Theatre: First Saturday per month enjoy astronomy learning and get to view the objects in space through the UNT telescopes at the Rafes Urban Astronomy Center.

- White Rock Lake: Show your love for the lake and volunteer at the Second Saturday Shoreline Spruce-Up Events (second Saturday/month).

My Favorite Day!

Sunday

- Dallas Heritage Village: Family Past Times on the first Sunday/ month. Kids are FREE the first Sunday of the each month.
- Meadows Museum of Art: Drawing from the Masters Program (15 and older)
- The Modern (Fort Worth): FREE!
- National Scouting Museum: Free admission on Sunday and Mondays
- Old Red Museum: Early Bird Special if tickets are purchased before noon.
- Trinity River Audubon Center: Nature Club on the third Sunday per month
- UNT Sky Theater: FREE parking

My Favorite Season: Spring!

April

- Air Power Expo (airpowerexpo.com): US Navy's Blue Angels show of aerial acrobatics in northwest Fort Worth.

- Arbor Daze (Euless, TX / arbordaze. org): Family friendly festival that promotes the planting of trees. Includes plant sales and rides for kids.

- Azalea & Spring Glower Trail (Tyler, TX / tylerazaleatrail.com): Tour residential gardens and enjoy plant sales. Check out local art among miles of azaleas and dogwoods in full bloom.

- Cedar Hill Earth Day (cedarhilltx.com): Environmentally conscious vendors, conservation workshops, farmer's market, and performances.

- Community Partners of Dallas (cpdtx. org): Check how you can get involved in Child Abuse Prevention Month.

- Dallas Arboretum: Dallas Blooms!

- Dallas Heritage Village: Plow, Plant and Shear/Girl Scout Day

- Dallas International Guitar Festival (guitarshow.com)

- Dallas Polo Club: Start of the outdoor season.

- Dallas Zoo: Frog Club starts monthly meetings and activities for ages 8+

- Deep Ellum Arts Festival (deepellumartsfestival.com): Free admission to an enormous street festival on six blocks of Main Street in Deep Ellum.

Spring Equinox
On the first day of spring, the vernal equinox, day and night are each approximately 12 hours long.

The Sun crosses the celestial equator going northward; it rises exactly due east and sets exactly due west.

Average Temp
(High / Low)
April: 77 / 56
May: 84 /65
June: 92 / 73

On average, the most precipitation in Dallas occurs in May.

My Favorite Season: Spring!

- Earth Day Texas (earthdaytx.org): Held annually in Fair Park. Free Admission and lots of exhibits.
- Frisco Fire Safety Town (Frisco, TX): Spring & Summer safety events from April - July.
- The Gentle Zoo (Forney, TX): Easter celebration and Easter egg hunt.
- Grapevine Vintage Railroad: Easter Bunny Train Ride
- Lake Cliff Park: Earth Day Celebration
- Mesquite Championship Rodeos
- Prairie Dog Chili Cook-off
- Sandy Lake Amusement Park: Check the schedule for the Fun Fest with elementary through high school orchestras, bands, and choirs competing for special prizes.

May

- Anita N. Martinez Ballet Folklorico: Check the schedule for the Educational Matinée Series.
- Cinco de Mayo Parade and Festival (dallascincodemayo.net): Parade and cultural festival held downtown.
- City Arts Festival (cityartsfestival.com): Activities and entertainment held annually in Fair Park.
- Cottonwood Art Festival (Richardson / cottonwoodartfestival.com): Semi-annual free event held in Cottonwood Park. Be sure to visit the Art Stop Children's Area.
- Crow Collection of Asian Art: Mid-May Merriment. Celebrate holidays and festivals from across the Asian continent.
- Fishin' Fun (Farmers Branch / farmersbranchtx.gov): Kids 16 and under can join in on the fun while fishing for the biggest catfish.
- Grapevine Main Street Festival (Grapevine/ grapevinetexas.org): Festival held along Main Street in Historic Grapevine. Includes a KidCave and carnival.
- MayFest (Fort Worth / mayfest.org): Family-friendly festival on 33 acres along the Trinity River in Fort Worth. Music, festival food, rides, and bounce houses galore.
- Scarborough Renaissance Festival: (srfestival.com) Thirty-five acres with over 24 stages and 200 unique acts.
- Wildflower! Arts and Music Festival (Richardson / wildflowerfestival.com): Gatalyn Park

Are We There Yet? Dallas

West Nile Virus

West Nile Virus is spread by the bite of an infected mosquito and can infect people, birds, and other animals. Most people infected with West Nile Virus will only have mild symptoms, such as headache, fever, and rash. People with a weakened immune system are at increased risk. Only about 1 in 150 people infected will develop a more serious form of the disease which could include muscle weakness, paralysis, or death.

West Nile Virus is commonly found in West Asia, Africa, and the Middle East. The Centers for Disease Control (CDC) estimate it has been in the United States since 1999.

In the summer of 2012, a record outbreak of the West Nile Virus created a state of emergency in North Texas. West Nile Virus continues to be a concern in the community and the North Dallas counties have increased the use of mosquito traps and sprays.

Preventing mosquito bites is the best way to avoid infection.

Defend: Apply mosquito repellent on skin and clothing

Dress: Wear long sleeves and pants when outside

Drain: Reduce mosquito breeding sites by eliminating standing water

Dusk to Dawn: Stay indoors from the period of dusk to dawn when mosquitoes are most active

If you or a family member experience the symptoms mentioned above, contact your doctor immediately.

My Favorite Season: Spring!

June

- The first week of June is National Fishing Week. Check the parks and lakes for special events.
- Beckert Park in Addison: Summer Series featuring outdoor symphonies.
- Community Partners of Dallas (cpdtx.org): Back to School Drive
- Crow Collection of Asian Art: On the third Fridays of March, June, and September enjoy the Crow Collection After Dark. Each free themed event includes music, dance, films, and tours.
- Juneteenth Celebrations (junettenth.com): The oldest nationally celebrated commemoration of the ending of slavery in the United States. Look for events at Fair Park, Old Settler's Park, and community centers throughout Dallas.
- Mesquite Championship Rodeo: Check the schedule for opening day
- Sandy Lake Amusement Park: Open during the week and the weekend for summer hours
- Texas Black Invitational Rodeo (aamdallas.org): Hosted by the African American Museum. Check website for seasonal details.
- Texas Discovery Gardens: Fangs! Annual Family Festival
- Trinity River and Audubon Center: Check out the website for details as I have seen free admission during the summer months in the past.

Fireflies

Fireflies, also called lightning bugs, are actually beetles.

Bioluminescence begins with the egg and is present throughout the entire life cycle. All eggs, larvae, and pupae are capable of producing light.

Fireflies use their light signals to "talk" to each other. Males flash to show their eligibility and females reply to indicate where their located.

Not all fireflies flash to communicate. People west of the Rockies often assume there aren't fireflies, but in many areas of the western United States, they just don't flash. On the other extreme, in Southeast Asia and the Great Smoky Mountains National Park, the Photinus carolinus species actually synchronize their flash signals.

My Favorite Season: Summer!

July

- Beckert Park (Addison): Summer Series featuring outdoor Jazz.
- Community Partners of Dallas (cpdtx. org): Back to School Drive
- Dallas Summer Musicals: Check the calendar for an exciting summer season.
- Fair Park: Freedom Fest on July 4th
- Frisco Fire Safety Town (Frisco): Spring & Summer safety events from April - July
- Frontiers of Flight: Moon Day offers unique experiments, exhibits, and access to the wonderful museum and children's discovery area
- Heritage Village: Old- Fashioned Fourth
- Independence Day Celebration (Farmers Branch, TX / farmersbranchtx. gov): Fireworks, bands, and free Kid Zone.
- Kaboom Town (addisontexas.net): Fourth of July extravaganza in Addison.
- Taste of Dallas (tasteofdallas.org): Culinary festival with art, Kid's Zone, and Fireworks.

August

- Beckert Park (Addison): Summer Series featuring outdoor Salsa
- Community Partners of Dallas (cpdtx. org): Back to School Drive
- Dallas Arboretum: Summer discounts often available. Check website for information.

Summer Solstice

On the first day of summer, the summer solstice, we enjoy the most daylight of the calendar year.

The Sun reaches its most northern point in the sky at local noon. After this date, the length of daylight starts to decrease.

Average Temp
(High / Low)
July: 96/77
August: 96/77
September: 89/77

My Favorite Season: Summer!

- Dallas Theatre Center (dallastheatercenter.org): Check the calendar for Neighborhood Nights.
- Taste & Tunes (Farmers Branch, TX / farmersbranchtx.gov): Food trucks and live music.
- Texas Discovery Gardens: Butterflies and Bugs! Annual Family Festival
- Viva Dallas! Hispanic Expo (gdhcc.com): Entertainment, art, health services (including free screenings), and more are held annually in the Dallas Market Hall.

September

- Connemara Meadow Preserve: Into the Meadow (For Adults)
- Crow Collection of Asian Art: On the third Fridays of March, June, and September enjoy the Crow Collection After Dark. Each free themed event includes music, dance, films, and tours.
- Dallas Arboretum: Over 50,000 pumpkins and squash transform the arboretum for fall. Enjoy hay maze, scavenger hunts, and the nationally acclaimed Pumpkin Village.
- Dallas Pride Parade (dallaspride.org): Started in 1972 as a small parade to commemorate the 1969 Stonewall Riots, the Dallas Pride Parade has grown over the years and now includes dozens of performances, events, and a Family Pride Zone (a welcoming place for LGBT parents and their kids).
- GrapeFest (grapevinetexasusa.com): The largest wine festival in the Southwest, offers children's activities and carnival rides.
- Greek Food Festival of Dallas (greekfestivalofdallas.com): Food, music, dancing, and designated Kids Area.
- International Museum of Cultures: Check the calendar to learn more about the Fall Festival which includes a series of guest speakers, films, dance, music, and art activities on Saturdays.
- North Texas Food Bank (NTFB.org): Hunger Action Month
- Plano Balloon Festival (planoballoonfest.org): Hot Air Balloon Festival, marathons, food, fireworks and more.
- Texas Home & Garden Show (texashomeandgarden.com): Largest home and garden show in Texas.
- Trinity River Audubon Center: Sign up for Nature Club which provides a monthly hands-on activity, science investigation and outdoor fun for kids ages 5-12.

My Favorite Season: Fall!

October

- Addison Octoberfest (addisontexas.net): More than 70,000 visitors come to enjoy German food, music, dancing, and entertainment.

- American Indian and Southwestern Art Market (indianmarket.net): Live music, art, food, and children's activities.

- Anita N. Martinez Ballet Folklorico: Check the schedule for the Educational Matinée Series.

- Big Orange Pumpkin Farm (Gunter / prestontrailfarms.com): Pick pumpkins off the vine. $8 admission includes one small pumpkin, feed for farm animals, hay maze, and hayride.

- Butterfly Flutterby (Grapevine / grapevinetexas.gov): Parade and celebration for the migration of the Monarch butterfly.

- Community Partners of Dallas (cpdtx. org): Coat Drive

- Cottonwood Art Festival (Richardson, TX / cottonwoodartfestival.com): Semi-annual free event held in Cottonwood Park. Be sure to visit the Art Stop Children's Area.

- Dallas Arboretum: Pumpkin Patch, Pumpkin Village, and hay bale maze.

- Dallas Firefighter's Museum: Celebrate National Fire Prevention Week. Also check out the sparky.org website for activities, games, checklists, and more provided by the National Fire Prevention Association.

- Dallas Symphony Orchestra: Halloween Organ Spooktacular

Fall Equinox
On the first day of fall, the autumnal equinox, day and night are each about 12 hours long.

The Sun crosses the celestial equator going southward; it rises exactly due east and sets exactly due west.

Average Temp
(High / Low)
October: 79/58
November: 67/48
December: 58/39

Who is the Biggest Cowboy?

In the free-wheeling years after the war, merchants in Kerens, Texas, had a problem. Residents of the tiny town were driving to nearby Corsicana or even 75 miles north to Dallas for their Christmas shopping sprees. Looking for a gimmick that might encourage people to spend money at local stores, the Kerens Chamber of Commerce built what they claimed was the world's largest Santa Claus, a 49-foot-tall figure constructed from iron-pipe drill casing and paper mache with 7-foot lengths of unraveled rope for a beard.

The promotion was a big success during the 1949 holidays, but the novelty wore off the following year, and community support waned.

In 1951, State Fair president R. L. Thornton purchased Santa's components for $750 and hired Dallas artist Jack Bridges to create a giant cowboy out of the material.

Big Tex made his debut at the 1952 State Fair of Texas. Wearing size 70 boots and a 75-gallon hat, Tex towered 52' above wide-eyed visitors at Fair Park. His denim jeans and plaid shirt were donated by the H. D. Lee Company of Shawnee Mission, Kansas. Cosmetic surgery the following year straightened his nose, corrected a lascivious wink, and allowed him to talk.

On October 19, 2012, Big Tex was destroyed by an electrical fire. Don't worry he was rebuilt in time for the opening day of the 2013 season with a replacement cost of $500,000.

> *The State Fair of Texas has been held in Dallas every year since 1886 with five exceptions.*
>
> *In 1918, the fair was canceled on account of WWI, and between 1942-1945 due to World War II.*

- Dallas Zoo: Boo at the Zoo
- Flower Mound Pumpkin Patch (flowermoundpumpkinpatch.com): $5 parking. Mazes for big and small, bounce houses, cartoon cutouts, pumpkin train, and playground equipment.
- Frisco Fire Safety Town (Frisco, TX): Offers a unique and safe trick-or-treat experience.
- The Gentle Zoo (Forney, TX): Pumpkin patch, petting zoo, mazes, and carnival games.
- Grapevine Vintage Railroad: Halloween Scream Train
- Halloween in the Park (Farmers Branch, TX / farmersbranchtx.gov)
- Pumpkins on the Prairie (Frisco / pumpkinsontheprairie.org): FREE! Bounce house, hayrides, maze, face painting, and games.
- Ripley's Believe It or Not! (Grand Prairie, TX): Special October late night events – Nightmare at the Wax Museum
- Six Flags Over Texas: Pet Parade
- State Fair of Texas (Fair Park / bigtex.com)
- Texas Discovery Gardens: Creepy Crawl-o-ween! Annual Family Festival
- Trinity River Audubon Center: Owl-O-Ween
- Tucker Hill Pumpkinville (McKinney / tuckerhilltx.com): FREE! Pumpkins for sale, but includes family friendly activities such as hayrides, games, toddler size maze, and music.
- Yester Land Farm (Canton / About an hour East on 1-20 / yesterlandfarm.com): Enjoy pumpkin patches, rides, corn maze, train rides, and a petting zoo.

November

- Community Partners of Dallas (cpdtx.org): Holiday Toy Drive
- Dallas Dance Festival (dallasdancefestival.com): Annual festival in the Arts District featuring emerging and upcoming dance companies.
- Dallas Heritage Village: Civil War on the Home Front
- Texas Red Nations Powwow (powwows.com)
- Texas Stampede Rodeo (Allen, TX / visitallen.com)
- Veterans Day Celebration (Farmers Branch / farmersbranchtx.gov)

December

- Big D NYE (bigdnye.com): New Year's Eve Party and countdown in Victory Park.

- Children's Health Holiday Parade (dallaschildrensparade.com)

- Christmas Boat Parade and Bonfire (Lynn Creek Park / joe-pool-lake. org): Boats lite up with Christmas lights and fireworks.

- Christmas in the Branch (Farmers Branch / farmersbranchtx.gov): Enjoy a tour of lights for free at Farmers Branch Historical Park.

- Community Partners of Dallas (cpdtx.org): Holiday Toy Drive

- Cotton Bowl Parade of Bands (cottonbowl.com): High school bands from across the nation.

- Dallas Arboretum and Botanical Gardens: 12 days of Christmas program.

- Dallas Heritage Village: Candlelight

- Dickens of a Christmas (McKinney / mckinneytexas.org): Downtown transforms into an old fashioned scene with horse-drawn carriages, carolers, lights, music, and food.

- Frisco Fire Safety Town (Frisco, TX): Holiday Lights program.

- Galleria Mall (North Dallas / galleriadallas.com): Ice Skating around the largest indoor Christmas tree in the nation.

- Gaylord Texan Resort & Convention Center (marriot.com): ICE! A winter wonderland with holiday scenes carved out of more than 2 million pounds of ice.

- Grapevine Vintage Railroad: North Pole Express

- Highland Park (hptx.org): Join the tradition that has been around since 1927 on the first Thursday in December at 7pm when the 140 year old pecan tree is lit with over 5,000 lights (corner of Preston Road and Armstrong Parkway).

- Majestic Theatre: Classic Nutcracker Ballet

- Myerson Symphony Center: Numerous holiday concerts and events.

- North Park Center (northparkcenter.com): See the tradition that started in 1987. More than 1,600 feet of track with 35 toy trains running through a miniature Dallas.

- Texas Ballet (texasballettheater.org): Check the website for availability of free performances of the Nutcracker.

- Twinkle Light Boat Parade (Grapevine / grapevinetexas.gov): Water crafts decorated with Christmas lights.

Are We There Yet? Dallas

My Favorite Season: Winter!

January

- Dallas Symphony Orchestra: Auditions for the Young Strings Program
- Dallas Zoo: Admission drops to $5
- Fair Park: New Year's Day Cotton Bowl
- Kid Film Festival (usafilmfestival.com): Film Festival appropriate for all ages.
- Martin Luther King Jr Parade (dallasblack.com): Marching bands, floats, drill teams, and dance troupes to commemorate the work and life of Martin Luther King Jr.
- MLK Day of Service: Look for volunteer opportunities in your community.
- Texas Home & Garden Show (texashomeandgarden.com)

Winter Solstice

The first day of winter is the darkest day of the year when the Sun reaches its most southern point in the sky at local noon.

After this date, the amount of daylight begins to increase.

Average Temp
(High / Low)
Jan.: 57/37
Feb. 61/41
March: 69/49

My Favorite Season: Winter!

February

- Autorama (autorama.com): Custom car show that pays tribute to innovative workmanship.
- Dallas Zoo: Admission drops to $5
- Russian Festival (smu.edu): Festival of music and art at SMU.

March

- Community Partners of Dallas (cpdtx.org): Easter Basket Drive
- Crow Collection of Asian Art: On the third Fridays of March, June, and September enjoy the Crow Collection After Dark. Each free themed event includes music, dance, films, and tours.
- Devil's Bowl Speedway: Check the website for the opening night and schedule.
- Greenville Avenue St. Patrick's Day Parade (greenvilleave.org): This parade started in 1979 and has grown to the largest St. Patrick's Day parade in the Southwest.
- Nasher Sculpture Center: Spring Break 'til Midnight is the perfect event for pre-teens and teens. Concert and movie held outdoors for FREE!
- North Texas Irish Festival (ntif.org): Music, food, and art to celebrate Irish and Celtic performance and heritage.
- Out of the Loop Fringe Festival (watertowertheatre.org/outofloop.aspx): Ten day festival packed with dance, music, and visual arts in Addison.

Best by Age

PreK and Under

- Bob Jones Nature Center (Southlake, TX): Pathfinders Outdoor Preschool is offered once per week for "independent" and potty trained 3 – 5 year olds. Babes in the Woods program is also available for ages 18 – 3 years plus adult.
- Children's Aquarium at Fair Park
- Crow Museum of Art: Yoginos and Young Dragons
- Dallas Arboretum and Botanical Gardens
- Dallas Angelika Film Center: Crybaby Matinée
- Dallas Children's Theater
- Dallas Heritage Village: "Nip and Tuck's Barnyard Buddy Stories" on the second Wednesday per month at 11am.
- Dallas Museum of Art: Art Babies; Toddler Art; Arturo's Art & Me; and First Tuesdays art activities
- Dallas Public Libraries
- Dallas World Aquarium
- Dallas Zoo
- Founder's Plaza Plane Observation Area
- Frontiers of Flight Museum
- The Gentle Zoo
- Grapevine Vintage Railroad
- Heritage Farmstead Museum
- Irving Arts Center
- Klyde Warren Park
- Lakeside Park
- Liberty Park
- Latino Cultural Center
- Nasher Sculpture Center
- Perot Museum of Nature and Science
- Pleasant Oaks Park
- Sandy Lake Amusement Park: $2 admission and super inexpensive kid friendly rides, golf, and pool tickets.
- Sea Life Grapevine Aquarium
- Surf and Swim (Garland): Great splash pad for the little ones with a low entry cost.
- Texas Discovery Gardens in Fair Park
- Trinity River Audubon Center
- UNT Sky Theater
- White Rock Lake

Best for Elementary Age Explorers

- Adventure Landing
- Bahama Beach Waterpark
- Bob Jones Nature Center
- Cedar Hill State Park & Joe Pool Lake
- Children's Aquarium at Fair Park
- Dallas Arboretum and Botanical Gardens
- Dallas Children's Theater
- Dallas Firefighter's Museum
- Dallas Museum of Art: Special Workshops and Classes and Summer Art Camp programs
- Dallas Opera
- Dallas Public Libraries
- Dallas Symphony Orchestra (DSO)
- Dallas World Aquarium
- Dallas Zoo: Be sure to check out the Family Nights and Family Camp options
- Dragon Park
- Fair Park
- Fine Arts Chamber Players (FACP)
- Frisco Fire Safety Town
- Frontiers of Flight Museum
- Galaxy Drive-In
- Grapevine Vintage Railroad
- Hawaiian Falls Adventure Park
- Heard Natural Science Museum and Wildlife Sanctuary
- Heritage Farmstead Museum
- Irving Arts Center
- Klyde Warren Park
- Kiest Park
- Lake Cliff Park
- Lakeside Park
- Latino Cultural Center
- Liberty Park
- Mesquite Championship Rodeo
- Nasher Sculpture Center
- National Scouting Museum
- Old Red Museum
- Perot Museum of Nature and Science
- Pleasant Oaks Park
- Ripley's Believe It or Not! (Grand Prairie)
- Sandy Lake Amusement Park
- Sea Life Grapevine Aquarium
- Six Flags Hurricane Harbor
- Six Flags Over Texas
- Speed Zone
- Texas Discovery Gardens in Fair Park
- Top Golf
- Trinity River Audubon Center
- Trinity River Expeditions
- UNT Sky Theater
- White Rock Lake

Best for Pre-Teens and Teens

- Adventure Landing
- Bob Jones Nature Center (Southlake, TX): Nature Photography Classes for 14 an up. The Camera Club is also available and meets the third Saturday of each month and holds critique sessions on the first Monday of the month. $20 -$35 annual membership fee. Also check on the Starstruck dates where you and your family can take advantage of some star gazing through the high powered telescope available at the center (free for members, $5 for non-members)
- Cedar Hill State Park & Joe Pool Lake
- Creative Arts Center of Dallas (East Dallas): Classes, workshops, and show opportunities for emerging artists
- Dallas Arboretum and Botanical Gardens
- Dallas Heritage Village: Junior Historians volunteer camp for ages 11 to 18
- Dallas Holocaust Museum
- Dallas International Guitar Festival (guitarshow.com): Huge annual guitar show at Fair Park. If you have young rockers, be sure to check out the TX10 under 20 competition guidelines early and enter to perform and win great prizes.
- Dallas Museum of Art: Concerts, Lectures, and Teen workshops. Also be sure to check the C3 Studio, C3 Tech Lab, and C3 Theater schedules.
- Dallas Opera
- Dallas Public Libraries
- Dallas Symphony Orchestra (DSO)
- Fair Park
- Fine Arts Chamber Players (FACP)
- Fort Paintball
- Frontiers of Flight Museum
- Galaxy Drive-In
- Hawaiian Falls Adventure Park
- Heard Natural Science Museum and Wildlife Sanctuary
- Heritage Farmstead Museum
- Klyde Warren Park
- Kiest Park
- Lake Cliff Park
- Lakeside Park
- Latino Cultural Center
- Main Event
- Meadows Museum of Art: Drawing from the Masters program
- Mesquite Championship Rodeo
- Nasher Sculpture Center: Free outdoor concerts and movies that run til midnight.

Best for Pre-Teens and Teens, continued

- Perot Museum of Nature and Science
- Pocket Sandwich Theatre
- Ripley's Believe It or Not! (Grand Prairie)
- Room Escape Adventures
- Sea Life Grapevine Aquarium
- Six Flags Hurricane Harbor
- Six Flags Over Texas
- Sixth Floor Museum at Dealey Plaza: Youth Advisory Committee
- Speed Zone
- Skyline Trapeze: Classes in flying trapeze, juggling, balance, and more.
- Top Golf
- Trinity Forest Aerial Adventure Park: Challenge yourself with military style courses, canopy tours, and zip lines.
- Trinity River Audubon Center
- Trinity River Expeditions
- White Rock Lake
- Zero Gravity: Big time thrill rides including bungee jumping and free fall amusements.

The BEST Birthday Party!

- Amazing Jake's Food and Fun
- Bahama Beach Waterpark
- Bob Jones Nature Center: Themed nature parties in the Nature Center or outside. $180 for 10 children; $15 for each additional child.
- Bounce U
- Children's Aquarium at Fair Park: Birthday party packages for up to 25 guests offered at set times on Saturdays and Sundays. Package cost is $350 and includes animal encounter, stingray feeding, party room, and tableware.
- Cosmic Jump
- Dallas Heritage Village: Time traveler, Texas Rangers, garden, and pioneer party options available.
- Dallas Zoo: Zoofari Birthday Party Package includes admission for 20 guests, use of the party room for 1.5 hours, and animal interaction. Cost is $475 for non-members / $425 for members.
- Dr Pepper Star Centers: Birthday party with ice skating – What could be better? Available for $125 and up at the Dr Pepper Star Centers. Parties include public skating admission and party table. Upgrades are available.
- Frontiers of Flight: Two hour party starts at $115, includes access to the wonderful children's area and the museum.
- The Gentle Zoo (Forney, TX): Two party package options ranging from $150 to $350 for up to 20 guests. Based on package, you can receive admission, party area, petting zoo, train ride, maze, and access to the playground.
- Hawaiian Falls Adventure Park
- Heard Natural Science Museum and Wildlife Sanctuary: Staff guides party activities and an outdoor hike. A live animal visits the party! $200 to $300
- Indoor Safari Park
- Lil Ninjas
- Lunar Mini Golf
- Main Event

- McKinney Avenue Transit Authority: Truly a unique party for ages 4 and up. Enjoy a chartered trolley ride ($200 for two hours).
- Perot Museum: Two options: Birthday at the Museum or Birthday at Your Place. Parties available on Saturdays and Sundays. Birthday at the Museum allows you to choose from a variety of themes appropriate for various age groups and party sizes. If booking Birthday at Your Place, a museum educator will come to your home, park, or reserved restaurant to engage and educate your guests for 45 minutes.
- Pole Position Raceway
- Pump It Up
- Ripley's Believe It or Not! (Grand Prairie): Birthday Party packages available. Call 972.263.2391 for additional information.
- Room Escape Adventures: Best for adventurous 14 and older group. Maximum size is 12.
- Sea Life Grapevine Aquarium
- Speed Zone: Packages start at $99
- Skyline Trapeze: Email skylinetrapeze@gmail.com or call 214.771.2406 for additional information. Classes in flying trapeze, juggling, balance, and more.

- Texas Discovery Gardens: Two themes available: Butterflies or Rain forests. Each party lasts two hours and includes setup, party room, and admission. Up to 40 guests. $212 - $250

- Texas Rangers Youth Ballpark: Plan an awesome birthday party for $125/hour (two hour minimum). The price includes a $50 food and beverage credit at the concession stands.

- Trinity Forest Aerial Adventure Park: Six and older with minimum height of 48". Challenge your party attendees with military style courses, canopy tours, and zip lines. Packages start at $260 for 10 participants.

- Trinity River Audubon Center: Birthday parties at the Audubon are one hour of educator-led outdoor investigations of birds, bugs or butterflies followed by an hour of cake and parent-led indoor activities. Call to reserve: 214.309.5812.

- Whirlyball and Laser Whirld (Plano): Laser tag or whirly ball/arcade packages available and start at $150. Includes pizza and drinks.

- Zero Gravity: Party packages available starting at $28 per person (minimum height is 42"/ minimum participants number is 10).

FREE ON YOUR BIRTHDAY

- Medieval Times Dinner & Tournament
- Frisco Rough Riders: Join Deuce's Birthday Club to receive a free ticket the month of your child's birthday

Are We There Yet? Dallas

The BEST Sleepover

In addition to the great camping opportunities in and around Dallas, check out some of these overnight options.

- Children's Aquarium at Fair Park: Sleep among five aquatic zones and thousands of fish. Includes a guided tour, activities and crafts, nighttime snack, and breakfast. Minimum age is 5. Cost is $40 per youth or adult.

- Dallas Zoo: Sleepovers include after-hour guided tours, behind the scenes activities and feeding demonstrations, late night snack, breakfast, and zoo entrance for the following day. The camp out beings at 7pm with a minimum participant age of 5. Adult cost is $65 – 80 and kids are $50 – 65 based on membership.

- Fossil Rim Wildlife Center: Cabins available starting at $85.

- Perot Museum: Designed for ages 6-12, the Perot sleepover allows for behind the scenes access to exhibits and exclusive demonstrations. Guests enjoy a 3D movie and light breakfast.

Are We There Yet? Dallas

The BEST Food

There are so many great restaurants to choose from in Dallas. ...is small list definitely does not represent them all, but was gathered with the help of friends when asked what are your favorite kid friendly restaurants.

DOWNTOWN

- **Café Strada**
  1520 Elm, Suite 107, Dallas 75203
  214.202.6485

  Located in front of the Joule Hotel in a pedestrian alleyway between Elm and Main, this little restaurant offers a charming patio in downtown. Coffee, smoothies, gelato, paninis, and salads are available.

- **Ellen's Southern Kitchen**
  1718 N Market Street, Dallas 75202
  469.206.3339
  ellenssouthernkitchen.com

  Southern and delicious Breakfast, Lunch, and Dinner with great service.

- **Yolk One Arts Plaza**
  1722 Routh Street, Dallas 75201
  214.855.9655
  eatyolk.com

  Creative breakfasts and specialty juices in an urban, upscale setting.

WEST DALLAS

- **Chicken Scratch**
  2303 Pittman Street, Dallas, 75208
  214.749.1112
  cs-tf.com

  "Slow fast food" served up in a family atmosphere. Great price points on fresh hormone free, local farm chicken and fresh garden food. Great outdoor dining space with live music on weekends.

- **Lockhart Smokehouse BBQ**
  400 W Davis Street, Dallas 75208
  214.944.5521
  lockhartsmokehouse.com

  Jill Grobowsky Bergus' grandfather ran the legendary Kreuz Market. With the help from family and Pitmaster Tim McLaughlin, the amazing flavor of Kreuz is in Dallas and Plano. No forks! No Sauce! Market sausage served on butcher paper.

- **Start**
  4023 Lemmon Ave, Dallas 75219
  214.599.7884
  startrestaurant.net

  Inspiring the community to eat better, even when on the road. From-scratch, delicious take-out food served in environmentally-friendly packaging.

UPTOWN & PARK CITIES

- **Chuy's**
  4544 McKinney Ave, Dallas 75205
  214.559.2489
  chuys.com

  Chuy's is a Tex-Mex chain that originated in Austin. Served fresh in a funky atmosphere.

- **Dough Pizzeria Napoletana**
  11909 Preston Road, Dallas 75230
  978.788.4600
  doughpizzeria.com

  Neapolitan style pizza and Southern Italian cuisine in a great casual neighborhood setting.

- **Dream Café**
  2800 Ruth Street, Suite 170, Dallas 75201
  214.954.0486
  thedreamcafe.com

  Excellent outdoor patio space with play areas. Serves up fresh, hormone free, and locally sourced food.

- **Highland Park Old Fashioned Soda Fountain**
  3229 Knox Street, Dallas 75205
  214.521.2126
  highlandparksodafountain.com

  One hundred plus year old Soda Fountain that still serves up excellent milk shakes, malts, grilled cheese sandwiches, and more.

- **Southpaw's Organic Grill**
  6009 Berkshire Lane, Dallas 75225
  214.987.0351
  southpawsgroup.com

  Healthy, organic and natural food without added sugars, syrups, nitrates, or preservatives. Additional locations in Gables Uptown Tower, Equinox Highland Park, and Equinox Preston Hollow.

- **Wild About Harry's**
  3113 Knox Street, Dallas 75205
  wildaboutharrys.com

  It's a family tradition to stop in for some frozen custard and hot dogs.

  After enjoying yourself at Wild About Harry's, be sure to stop in at Froggie's 5 & 10 (3211 Knox Street). They have an excellent book and toy selection in this great retail shop.

NORTH DALLAS

- **Babe's Chicken Dinner House**
  1006 W. Main Street, Carrollton, 75006
  972.245.7773

  1456 Beltline Road, Suite 171, Garland, 75044
  972.496.1041

  babeschicken.com

  Amazing friend chicken and plentiful side dishes. Friendly staff in a casual atmosphere were children are always welcome.

The BEST Food

- **Dream Café** (Addison / In the Village on the Parkway)
  5100 Belt Line Road, Suite 732, Dallas,
  972.503.7326
  thedreamcafe.com

  Excellent outdoor patio space with play areas. Serves up fresh, hormone free, and locally sourced food.

- **Keller's Drive-In**
  6537 E Northwest Hwy (near Abrams Rd), Dallas 75231
  214.368.1209

  Fantastic shakes, onion rings, poppy seed buns, and hickory sauce put this old time drive-in on the map. The quick, friendly service will bring you back in time and so will the classic cars as many enthusiasts gather here.

- **Kirin Court**
  221 W Polk Street, Richardson, 75081
  214.575.8888
  kirincourt.com

  Family style authentic Chinese, Dim Sum, and Vegetarian cuisine. Pick freshly made dishes off wheeled carts and savor the surprise.

- **Lockhart Smokehouse BBQ (Plano)**
  1026 East 15th Street, Plano 75074
  972.516.8900
  lockhartsmokehouse.com

  Jill Grobowsky Bergus' grandfather ran the legendary Kreuz Market. With the help from family and Pitmaster Tim McLaughlin, the amazing flavor of Kreuz is in Dallas and Plano. No forks! No Sauce! Market sausage served on butcher paper.

- **Magic Time Machine**
  5003 Belt Line Road, Dallas 75254 (Addison)
  972.980.1903
  magictimemachine.com

  Costumed characters serve steaks, prime rib, and seafood in a 'funky nostalgic building.

EAST DALLAS

- **Café Silva**
  8499 Greenville Ave, Suite 108, Dallas 75231
  214.267.9836
  cafesilva.com

  Café Silva is located a few feet from White Rock Creek at the
  intersection of Royal Lane and Greenville Avenue. From White Rock
  Trail, take the side path near the soccer fields at Northwood Park.
  This cozy, locally owned coffee house serves espresso, pastries, and
  sandwiches.

- **Crossroads Diner**
  8121 Walnut Hill Lane, Suite 100, Dallas, 75231
  214.346.3491
  crossroads-diner.com

  Fresh ingredients are used to make the great recipes. Specializing
  in an awesome breakfast. Served in a comfortable, casual, and kid
  friendly environment. Join the Sticky Buns Club to get a special
  delicious treat for your birthday, anniversary, and as a first timer.

- **Start**
  4814 Greenville Ave, Dallas 75206
  214.265.1411
  startrestaurant.net

  Inspiring the community to eat better, even when on the road. From-
  scratch, delicious take-out food served in environmentally-friendly
  packaging.

- **Truck Yard**
  5624 Sears Street, Dallas 75206
  469.500.0139
  texastruckyard.com

  Great outdoor dining on old style patio furniture and picnic tables.
  Multiple food trucks, delicious cheesesteak, ice cream, and a great
  atmosphere.

Are We There Yet? Dallas

The BEST Volunteer Experience

- Bob Jones Nature Center (Southlake, TX): Sign up to be a garden groomer, greeter, project prepper, or to help feeding the birds. The whole family can help by being a recycling buddy. Save salad and spinach containers, newspaper, and more for good use at the Center.

- Cedar Ridge Preserve: Consider putting the family to work on the trail or in the butterfly gardens. The third Saturday per month is Habitat Restoration and Trail Maintenance time. Tools, snacks, and water are provided. Contact info_CRP@yahoo.com for more information.

- Children's Health (childrens.com/get-involved/volunteer): Opportunities for group events, donations, and parade volunteering.

- Community Partners of Dallas (cpdtx.org): Amazing nonprofit that helps bring hope and healing to neglected and abused children in the Dallas area. Volunteer opportunities for teens, adults, and groups. Also be sure to check out and assist with the signature drives:
  - March: Easter Basket Drive
  - April: Child Abuse Prevention Month
  - June – August: Back to School Drive
  - October: Change is good month (coat drive)
  - November – December: Holiday Toy Drive.

- Dallas Arts District (thedallasartsdistrict.org): Volunteer as a docent, for special events, and apply for internships.

- Dallas Children's Theater (DCT):
  13+: Usher opportunities;
  16+: Office work and special project options.

- Dallas Heritage Village: Junior Historians volunteer summer camp for ages 11 to 18.

- Dallas Holocaust Museum / Center for Education and Tolerance: Volunteer opportunities, including design your own projects, are welcomed and encouraged. Contact: volunteer@ dallasholocaustmuseum.org.

- Dallas Parks and Recreation (dallasparks.org): Multiple opportunities throughout the Dallas Parks and Recreation Department to get involved throughout the city.

The BEST Volunteer Experience

- Dallas Public Libraries: Options for teens to start programs, host workshops, start a book club, etc.
- Dallas Zoo
  - Junior Zookeeper: Ages 11-12 (Program Fee $60)
  - Conservation Guide: Ages 13-18 (Program Fee $60)
  - Aquarium Guide: Ages 14-18 (Program Fee $60)
  - Junior Camp Counselor: Ages 14-18 (Program Fee $20)
- Fossil Rim Wildlife Center: Junior docents program is available for children 11 to 17 years.
- Frisco Fire Safety Town (Frisco): Daily and special events volunteer opportunities for ages 15 and up.
- Gardeners in Community Development (gardendallas.org): No minimum age. Provides fresh fruit and vegetables to low-income Dallas-area families from community gardens.
- Habitat for Humanity (dallasareahabitat.org/web/guest/youthprograms) : Youth Programs provide opportunities for children ages 5 and up to be engaged in bi-monthly activities and quarterly events.
- Latino Cultural Center: Docent, special events, and office duty volunteer positions for 18 and older.
- Lemons to Aid (lemonstoaid.org): Great ideas and opportunities for children of all ages to get involved in charitable giving. Hosts special fund raiser events that kids can help with and enjoy.
- Lewisville Lake Environmental Learning Area (ias.unt.edu/llela/main): Preservation and Restoration Volunteer Opportunities for elementary and high school age children.
- Meetup/Random Acts of Kindness (meetup.com/randomacts): Learn about new volunteer opportunities through the Random Acts of Kindness site on meetup, a social media type setting.
- North Texas Food Bank (NTFB.org): Founded in 1982, the NTFB now provides nearly 175,000 meals per day. Mark your calendar: September is Hunger Action Month. Volunteer information available on website. Options available for youth volunteers – minimum age varies by opportunity.
- Sixth Floor Museum at Dealey Plaza: Youth Advisory Committee invites 7th – 12th grade students to serve as ambassadors at special Museum functions, programs, and events.

- SoupMobile (soupmobile.com): The SoupMan and SoupTeam serve food to the homeless in an outdoor mobile feeding operation. Opportunities available for families.

- Studio Bella (studiobellaforkids.com): Kids going into 7th grade or older have volunteer opportunities to work with children in art and creativity classes.

- Susan G. Komen Breast Cancer Foundation, Inc. National Office (komen.org): Since 1982, Susan B. Komen for the Cure® has been funding research grants and community based outreach projects that focus on breast health education, screening, and treatment for medically underserved.

- TeenLife (teenlife.com): Provides listing of community service opportunities for teens.

- Texas Scottish Rite Hospital (tsrch.org/junior-volunteer-program): The Bernice and Budus Meyerson Junior Volunteer Program consists of two, five-week summer sessions that offer a wide range of opportunities for volunteers ages 14 to 17.

The BEST Volunteer Experience

- Trinity River Audubon Center: Habitat Restoration Day is a really interesting and educational volunteer opportunity for children 11 years and older. It is held the second Saturday of every month from 9am to 12pm. Becoming a Butterfly Gardener or joining a Special Events Team may be other great options for family volunteer opportunities.

- United Way (unitedwaydallas.org): Check out the calendar of events for family friendly opportunities at a variety of non-profit organizations.

- VNA Meals on Wheels (Vnatexas.org/our-services/meals-on-wheels): VNA provides compassionate private care services as well as hospice for people who are facing a final illness and provides the Meals on Wheels program in Dallas. In addition to volunteering to deliver meals, there are special projects in which individuals, friends, and families can contribute. Consider making Positive Place-mats with a warm message for Meals on Wheels clients.

- Wee Volunteer (weevolunteer.org): Provides age appropriate service projects for preschool and elementary school age children. Serves six areas of need: hunger; homelessness; under-privileged children; elderly; animals; and the environment.

- White Rock Lake (whiterocklake.org): Volunteer with the Friends of the Lake by adopting a shoreline, participating in the Second Saturday Shoreline Spruce-Up events, or many other options to support the lake.

- Volunteer Match (volunteermatch.org): National volunteer matching site that includes kid filter to make it easier to find age appropriate opportunities.

- Volunteer Now (volnow.org): Provides listings of volunteer needs from local non-profits. Volunteer Now recognizes that volunteering is for everyone and that when kids learn to do things for others, they develop a strong work ethic and a sense of community responsibility.

Art & Museums

Introduction

The Dallas Arts District

Dallas has the largest downtown arts and recreation complex in any US city. The transformation started in the 1970s when city officials set their minds on being a world class arts and culture destination. Over the next 40 years, development of the Arts District continued. Currently, the Dallas Arts District has 68 acres of downtown real estate dedicated to the arts.

Visit www.thedallasartsdistrict.org to schedule an exterior and history tour, see special events calendar, or sign up for volunteer opportunities (docents, special events, and internships).

Transportation: Parking is available in many locations with a starting price of $5. However, you can reduce the stress of downtown driving and parking concerns by taking DART with convenient stops at Pearl Street and St. Paul Street.

Pritzker Architecture Prize

When the new Winspear Opera House (Foster and Partners) and Wyly Theatre (Office for Metropolitan Architecture - Rem Koolhaas) join the existing Nasher Sculpture Center (Renzo Piano) and Meyerson Symphony Center (I.M. Pei and Partners), Dallas will be the only city in the world that has four buildings within one contiguous block that are all designed by Pritzker Architecture Prize winners.

Modeled after the Nobel Prize, the Pritzker Architecture Prize is internationally awarded each year to a living architects for significant achievement. The prize was established by Jay A. Pritzker with his wife, Cindy, through their Hyatt Foundation in 1979. As native Chicagoans, they were keenly aware of architecture and hoped their prize would encourage creativity and stimulate awareness of buildings.

Sources for Art & Museums Discounts and Events

- **Blue Star Museums**
  arts.gov/national/bluestartmuseums
  Many Dallas Museums participate in the Blue Star Museums
  Program. This national program provides discounts or free
  admission to active-duty military personnel and their families from
  Memorial Day through Labor Day.

- **City of Dallas Office of Cultural Affairs (OCA)**
  dallasculture.org
  OCA works to enhance the vitality of the City and the quality of
  life for all Dallas citizens. Through support and partnership for the
  23 city-owned facilities, OCA helps create environments where art
  and culture thrive. If you are looking for something creative and
  educational, be sure to check the website for current events.

- **Dallas City PASS**
  citypass.com/dallas
  Purchase a CityPASS to get admission tickets to four tourist
  attractions in Dallas and save 41% of the regular box office price.

- **KERA**
  artandseek.org / 90.1 FM
  Keep an eye on the excellent Art and Seek schedule provided by
  KERA, a national public radio affiliate station for North Texas.

- **Kids Club**
  Kids Club is a partnership between the Crow Collection of Asian Art,
  Dallas Zoo, Perot Museum, Nasher, Trinity River Audubon, and the
  Dallas Museum of Art. You can join the Kids Club at any of these
  organizations.
  Kids Club membership comes with special benefits and discounts
  from all six organizations.

AFRICAN AMERICAN MUSEUM

Fair Park
3536 Grand Avenue,
Dallas 75210

214.565.9026

aamdallas.org

Admission is FREE!

Hours
Tuesday – Friday:
11am to 5pm
Saturday: 10am to 5pm

Holidays
Closed: New Year's
Day, Independence
Day, Thanksgiving,
Christmas Eve, and
Christmas

The 38,000 square foot structure is home to a rich history of African American Art. The museum includes four galleries, a research library, a theatre, classrooms, and a sculpture garden. The permanent collections include African Art, African American fine art, magazines, and historical and political archives.

The African American Museum is home to one of the largest African American Folk Art collections in the U.S., featuring works from Clementine Hunter, David Butler, George White, Mose Tolliver, Sister Gertrude Morgan, Bessie Harvey, and Willard "The Texas Kid" Watson.

Your family may enjoy some of the wonderful special events offered, such a wellness fairs and art activities. Check out the website for additional information. Contact info@aamdallas.org for information on group tours.

THE ANN AND GABRIEL BARBIER-MUELL
MUSEUM: THE SAMURAI COLLECTI

The museum was created to house Ann and Gabriel Barbier-Mueller's ever expanding collection of Japanese armor. With over 1,000 objects, it is one of the largest samurai collections in the world. The armor, helmets, masks, and weaponry are rotated twice annually to present new opportunities for discovery.

This very small, hard to find, museum is definitely worth the trip and effort. Consider stopping in at the Saint Ann Restaurant for a bite, then popping upstairs to make the trip seem more like a true outing.

Near Victory Park
2501 North Harwood St., Dallas 75201

Above the Saint Ann Restaurant / Complimentary valet located at Harwood St. and Moody St. across the street from the Saint Ann's School building

214.965.1032

samuraicollection.org

Admission is FREE!

Hours
Monday: Closed
Tuesday: 11am to 8pm
Wednesday - Saturday: 11am to 6pm
Sunday: 11am to 5pm

BATH HOUSE CULTURAL CENTER

East
White Rock Lake
521 East Lawther,
Dallas 75218

214.670.8749

dallasculture.org

Admission is FREE!
(Gallery and museum
access. Theater prices
vary by performance.)

Hours
Tuesday - Saturday:
Noon to 6pm
Open to 10pm on
nights with theater
performances.

The Bath House Cultural Center building is an art-deco gem situated on the shores of White Rock Lake. It was built in 1930, providing lockers, changing rooms, and concessions to those who came to swim at the lake. When swimming discontinued in 1953, the building sat vacant for the next 25 years. After art activists urged the City of Dallas to restore the building, it opened to the public as the city's first neighborhood cultural center in 1981.

Currently, the 120 seat theater hosts a variety of performances and there are three gallery spaces which usually have local art on display. In addition, you can learn about the history of the lake and see great pictures of natives sunning themselves in what used to be the "beach" area in the small White Rock Lake Museum.

CROW COLLECTION OF ASIAN A

The Crow Collection of Asian Art was opened by Trammel and Margaret Crow in 1998 as a way to share their love of Asian art and culture. The collection includes more than 750 scrolls, paintings, and architectural pieces from China, Japan, India, and Southeast Asia. The center is surrounded by a lush sculpture garden.

Children two and older can participate in Yoginos, a trilingual (English, Spanish, and Sanskirt) yoga for youth program with sessions held in the gallery and Klyde Warren Park every Saturday from 11-11:45. Cost is $15 for the public, $10 for Crow Collection members, FREE for Wellness members. Space is limited, mats are provided. For more information, call 214.979.6438.

For those more interested in ninjas than yoga, there is also a Young Dragons program the first Saturday per month from noon to 1 pm. Kids can enjoy shuriken (throwing stars), katana (sword), bully proofing, and ninja balance. Free, but requires advance online registration.

For a full family event, be sure to stop in on the first Saturday per month from 10am – 2pm for Adventure Asia which includes face painting, storytelling, and art activities. Register online in advance.

Studio Saturdays are also held the second Saturday per month from 10am – 2pm. This hands-on art class is open to kids of all ages. Free for friends of the Crow Collection, $10 for the public. Space is limited, art supplies are provided. For more information, call 214.979.6438.

Downtown
2010 Flora St,
Dallas 75201

214-979-6430

crowcollection.org

Admission is FREE!

Hours
Monday: Closed
Tuesday – Thursday:
10am to 9pm
Friday & Saturday:
10am to 6pm
Sunday: Noon to 6pm

DALLAS CONTEMPORARY

West of Downtown
161 Glass Street,
Dallas 75207

214.821.2522

**dallascontemporary.
org**

Admission: FREE!

Hours
Tuesday – Saturday:
11am to 6pm
Sunday: Noon to 5pm

Dallas Contemporary is a non-profit that provides challenging regional, national, and international exhibitions, lectures, and educational programs.

DALLAS HERITAGE VILLA
AT OLD CITY PA

Known as "Old City Park" from its conception in 1969, visitors were often confused and expected a traditional park. Although the Dallas Heritage Village is located on the 13 wooded acres where Dallas' first city park and first zoo were located, it now offers much more than a traditional park. To better illustrate what is in store for visitors The Dallas Heritage Village took its new name in 2005.

The Dallas Heritage Village is home to the largest collection of 19th century pioneer and Victorian homes and commercial buildings in Texas. There are also more than 24,000 objects, including tools and implements, furnishings, domestic accessories, photographs, and postcards that represent the period of 1840-1910.

Dallas Heritage Village provides a variety of programs for all ages. Some programs are seasonal, while other offer opportunity for learning throughout the year. Be sure to drop in on the first Sunday of the month, when admission for children is FREE and the village hosts hands-on activities during their "Family Past Times" events. Little ones will also enjoy the "Nip and Tuck's Barnyard Buddy Stories" on the second Wednesday per month at 11am.

Downtown
1515 South Harwood Street, Dallas 75215

214.413.3679

dallasheritage village.org

Admission
Adults $9 / Senior $7
Children (4 to 12) $5
*Kids are free the first Sunday of the month

Hours
Tuesday – Saturday:
10am to 4pm
Sunday: Noon to 4pm
Closed: January and August

Holidays
Closed: Thanksgiving Day; Christmas Eve; Christmas Day; New Year's Eve; and New Year's Day

Guided-tours of two areas, Millermore and Sullivan, are offered daily at 1:30 p.m. and are included with museum admission. With little ones in mind, be sure to linger at the Learning Lounge which provides a great interactive play space.

The Village also offers party programs, Girl and Cub Scout workshops, and a junior historian's summer camp. Check the website for details on these as well as seasonal events, some of which are also listed in the Best of the Big D chapter in this book.

There are no restaurants on site, but snacks and drinks are available at the ticket office. Picnic lunches are welcome and recommended.

DALLAS HOLOCAUST MUSEUM
CENTER FOR EDUCATION AND TOLERANCE

Downtown / Historic West End District
211 N. Record St., Suite 100
Dallas 75202

214.741.7500

dallasholocaust museum.org

Admission
Adults: $10
Seniors, Students, Children, & Military: $8

Hours
Monday – Friday: 9:30am to 5pm
Saturday & Sunday: 11am to 5pm

Holidays
Closed: New Year's Day; Easter Sunday; Independence Day; Rosh Hashanah (2 Days); Yom Kippur; Thanksgiving Day; Christmas Eve; and Christmas Day

The museum was founded in 1984 and includes a core exhibit, museum archives and library, and special exhibits which often include guests and holocaust survivors scheduled to speak. The Museum is one of 19 Holocaust-related Museums in the United States. It is the only Holocaust Museum serving North Central Texas which is home to about 125 survivors and refugees.

The Core Exhibit focuses on one day during the Holocaust – April 19, 1943. On this day, three important events occurred: The 20th Deportation Train from Mechlin, Belgium was attached by partisans; The Warsaw Ghetto Uprising began; and the Bermuda Conference met. Artfully woven together, the happenings from these three very different events illustrate heroism, resistance, and appreciation for the strength and perseverance to overcome brutality and hatred.

Volunteer opportunities, including the opportunity to design your own project, are welcomed and encouraged. One such project resulted in the Garden of Remembrance built by Brandon Ryan and community volunteers. The unique steel sculpture garden is located at the northwest corner of Houston and Pacific Streets. For more information on volunteering, send a message to volunteer@dallasholocaustmuseum.org.

Additional Location Notes:
DART: West End Station to Record Street. Turn Left on Record Street & the museum will be on the corner of Record and Pacific.
Parking: Record and Houston St. Fee of $5 and up.
Wheelchair Accessible and strollers are welcome. Use entrance approximately 50 feet from main entrance with elevators inside.

DALLAS MUSEUM OF ART

In addition to the 10,000 priceless paintings and sculptures, a wonderful outdoor sculpture garden featuring Rodin, Moore, and others, the Dallas Museum of Art offers jazz concerts, "Object Slams", gallery talks, and Family Celebrations.

Take advantage of the Center for Creative Connections (C3). C3 includes interactive galleries, program spaces for kids, community projects, and visiting artist programs. Be sure to watch the calendar for Pop-Up Art Spots which provide a hands-on art experience for children. And if you have a teen or tween, be sure to monitor the C3 Studio, C3 Tech Lab, and C3 Theater schedule for creative opportunities.

If you have kids five and under be sure to mark your calendar for the First Tuesday series which includes art making, story times, performances, and gallery tours. First Tuesday is usually held from 11am – 2pm and a reasonably priced kid-friendly lunch is available. There are also multiple art classes and workshops, family film dates, a Yoga for kids program, and excellent bedtime story sessions told by award winning storyteller, Ann Marie Newman.

For more information about programs for young children, please visit the Dallas Museum of Art Family Page or call the museum.

Additional Location Notes:
Food is available at the DMA Café from 11am-4pm. The museum store is open the same hours as the museum. All public galleries and restrooms are ADA accessible.

Downtown
1717 North Harwood
Dallas 75201

214.922.1200

dma.org

Admission is FREE!
Special Exhibition
Admission:
Adults: $16
Seniors, Military, and
Students: $12
Children 11 and under:
FREE!

Hours
Closed on Mondays
Tuesday - Sunday
11am to 5pm
Thursdays:
Open until 9pm

Check out the museum calendar for special evening events on select Thursdays as well as the Late Night events held on the third Friday per month (except December) when the museum stays open until midnight.

Holidays
Closed: Thanksgiving Day; Christmas Day' and New Year's Day

GEOMETRIC MADI MUSEUM

Uptown
3109 Carlisle Street,
Dallas 75204

214.855.7802

**geometricmadi
museum.org**

Admission is FREE!

Hours
Monday: Closed
Tuesday – Saturday:
11am to 5pm
Thursday:
11am to 7pm
Sunday: 1 to 5pm

Carmelo Arden Quin articulated the ideas of the MADI movement in his MADI Manifesto (Buenos Aires, 1946). Some say the letters MADI stand for Materialismo Dialectismo (Dialectical Materialism). Others say it stands for Movimiento Artistico De Invencion.

Regardless of what MADI stands for, the art provides geometric delights that surprises, captivates, and amuses. The Geometric MADI Museum will do the same for your family, with fascinating design both inside and out.

Artists from Europe, Russia, Japan, South America, and the United States are represented in the museum. Visit regularly as new exhibits are available multiple times per year.

Workshops are available for children in kindergarten through college. Students receive instruction on using color, space, design, and shapes as they create their own three-dimensional projects. Classes are $5 per student.

GOSS-MICHAEL FOUNDATION

The Goss-Michael Foundation is dedicated to contributing to Dallas's art community. Stimulating exhibits are rotated on a quarterly basis throughout the year.

The Foundation also has a resource center available for use by aspiring young artists and started a scholarship program in 2007.

Watch the site for special events, such as Saturday Sketch days.

Northwest of Downtown
1405 Turtle Creek Boulevard, Dallas 75207

214.696.0555

gossmichael foundation.org

Admission is FREE!
Free parking behind the building

Hours
Tuesday & Friday: 10am to 5pm
Saturday: 11am to 4pm

HERITAGE FARMSTEAD MUSEUM

Far North / Plano
1900 West 15th Street
(Normal F. Whitsitt
Parkway/TX-FM544),
Plano 75075

972.881.0140

heritagefarmstead.org

Admission
Adults:
$3 (self-guided) /
$5 (docent guided)
Senior:
$3 (self-guided) /
$3.50 (docent guided)

Children 2 and under:
FREE!

Hours
Monday: Closed
Tuesday – Sunday:
10am to 4:30pm

Holidays
Closed: New Year's
Eve; New Year's Day;
Good Friday; Easter
Sunday; Independence
Day; Thanksgiving
Day; Thanksgiving
Friday; Christmas Eve;
and Christmas Day

The Heritage Farmstead Museum is located on the land of the 1891 farmhouse built by Hunter Farrell, a successful business man in Collin County. The farm was managed by Mary Alice Farrell and her daughter Ammie until 1972 when Ammie passed. After a seven-year, 1.2 million dollar restoration project, the Heritage Farmstead Museum opened to the public.

The 4.5 acre historic farm complex has been awarded designation by the Plano Landmark Association, a State of Texas Historical marker, and a listing in the National Register of Historic Places. The Heritage Farmstead Association has received accreditation from the prestigious American Association of Museums.

The Heritage Farmstead Museum contains 10,000 objects and archival materials. These objects relate to Blackland Prairie life in North Texas from the 1890 to 1920. The vast collection is used to furnish the Museum's historic buildings.

Docent Guided Tours are available Tuesday – Saturday at 10:30 and Sundays at 1:30. Reservations are required for guided tours with parties of six or more (call 972.881.0140).

Self-guided tours include the grounds, animal viewing, and the outside of the buildings. Self-guided tours do not include access to the Farrell-Wilson House, the Young House, or the School House. However, a printed guide is provided.

"Fun on the Farm Fridays" includes literacy-based programs, fun crafts, and a wagon ride geared towards children 18 months to five years. The program is for a parent/child couple and is available every Friday from 10:30 am to 12pm ($11 for one parent and one child, $6 per additional child, $3 per additional adult).

Heritage Farmstead Museum also offers unique opportunities for Girl Scouts, Boy Scouts, and PreK through Grade 6 field trips and learning programs. For children ages 6-12, the museum offers two summer camps that include outside play, scientific exploration at the creek, and learning about pioneer life.

INTERNATIONAL MUSEUM OF CULTURES

**Southwest /
Duncanville**
411 US 67 Frontage
Road,
Duncanville 75137

972.572.0462

**international
museumofcultures.org**

Admission
Adults: $5
Children, Students,
and Seniors: $4
Children 3 and under:
FREE

Hours
Monday - Friday:
10am to 6pm
Saturday:
Noon to 4pm

Duncansville is about 15 minutes southwest of Downtown Dallas. To get to the International Museum of Cultures take US 67 to the Danieldale Road exit and drive south on the access (frontage) road.

The small museum is dedicated to showing the cultural diversity of countries around the world. Learn more about the myths and legends of Ireland. Discover how the Yi or Lolo people farm in the mountainous regions of China. Expose your children to the rich and diverse languages of Mexico. Visit the Gallery to see collections from Texas artists.

Check the website for free days and educational program offerings.

IRVING ARTS CENTER

Opened in 1990, the Irving Arts Center's 10-acre complex provides a versatile performing and fine arts facility. There are two theaters, four galleries, a verdant sculpture garden, and meeting/classroom/reception areas.

The galleries include both permanent works and temporary installations. The sculpture garden is two-acres created to showcase regional artists.

Year-round youth and family programs are available and include story times, live performances, and summer camps.

Be sure to check the schedule for Family Fundays held regularly on the weekends. Fundays give parents and children a chance to co-create art projects using gallery exhibitions as inspiration.

Far West / Irving
3333 North MacArthur Blvd.
Irving 75062

972.252.7558

irvingartscenter.com

Admission
Gallery Admission and parking are FREE! Check the website for performance costs and times.

Hours
Gallery:
Monday - Saturday:
9am to 5pm
Thursday:
Open until 8pm
Sunday: 1 to 5pm

INO CULTURAL CENTER

Downtown
2600 Live Oak Street,
Dallas 75204

214.671.0045

dallasculture.org/
latinoculturalcenter

Admission is FREE!
Some events require a
fee. Check in advance
of visit.

Hours
Monday: Closed
Tuesday – Saturday:
10am to 5pm
Sunday: Closed

The Latin Cultural Center (LCC) includes an art gallery, a 300 seat theater, sculpture courtyard, and an outdoor plaza. The expansive courtyard is often used for cultural festivals including Dieciseis de Septiembre to Las Posadas. The art exhibits rotate every few months so plan to stop in often.

The fabulous 27,000 square foot facility was designed by renowned Mexican architect, Ricardo Legorreta and his son Victor. The brightly colored tower, plaza, and pyramid-like building pay tribute to Latin American traditions.

Tours are available and free, but reservations must be made four weeks in advance. Contact LCC for reservations and additional group opportunities. Educational field trips are also available and a variety of curriculum designed for grades 3-12 are available on the LCC website.

Check the events calendar on a regular basis and join the center's Facebook page for updates as the Latino Cultural Center can rightfully boost to hosting more than 300 music, dance, theater, and other cultural events a year. In addition, there are many offering for educational classes that will delight your children.

Be sure to mark your calendar for the Target Second Saturday events designed for the entire family. Each of these events provides a unique offering which may include stories, arts and crafts workshops, dance performances, and more.

If you are looking for a summer camp, the LCC has an offering for 5-8th graders. The camp provides the opportunity to work with trained artists while embracing the theater, creative writing, dance, cinematography, culinary art, and visual art. The program includes a final student performance.

Mexican Independence Day, September 16th

Every year on the 16th of September the President of Mexico addresses the Mexican people from the balcony of the National Palace to ring in a new year of independence in Mexico. By delivering a modern version of the famous Grito de Dolores, the President reminds the Mexican people of the movement started by Miguel Hidalgo in 1810 that lead to Spain recognizing Mexico's independence in 1836.

Mexican Independence is often confused with Cinco de Mayo. However, Cinco de Mayo celebrates the victory the Mexican army had over French troops in 1862.

MEADOWS MUSEUM OF ART

North of Highland Park
5900 Bishop Boulevard,
Dallas 75205

214.768.2516

**meadowsmuseum
dallas.org**

Admission
Adults: $10
Seniors: $8
Students: $4
Children 12 and under:
FREE!
FREE admission on
Thursdays after 5pm

Hours
Monday: Closed
Tuesday – Friday:
10am to 5pm
Thursdays:
Open until 9pm
Saturday: 10am to 5pm
Sunday: 1pm to 5pm

Holidays
Closed: Easter; July 4;
Labor Day; Thanks-
giving; Christmas Eve;
Christmas Day; and
New Year's Day

Inspired by his time spent at the Prado Museum in Madrid, Texas philanthropist and oil financier, Algur H. Meadows started his own collection of Spanish art in the late 1950s.

In 1962, he gave Southern Methodist University (SMU) the funds needed to build a museum to house his collection. After Mr. Meadows passed away in 1978, the Meadows Foundation continued to generously support the growth of an extraordinary collection, expanded educational programs, and a new museum building.

In 2015, The Meadows Museum celebrated its 50th anniversary. Currently, the Meadows houses one of the largest collections of Spanish art outside of Spain. The four major collections include early Renaissance to modern works, covering thousands of years of Spanish culture. The museum includes a plaza and sculpture garden.

Tour programs, special exhibits, and concerts are offered. Weekend family days as well as the summer art programs will delight both young and old.

The Drawing from the Masters program is free with admission and open to adults and students ages 15 and older. These informal afternoon classes, offered every other Sunday, provide drawing instruction.

Additional Location Notes:
Parking is free for museum visitors. Dart: Mockingbird Station – West on Mockingbird for about ¾ mile. Right on Bishop Boulevard. 1st building on right.

Wheelchair Accessible: Undergoing plans to make the space and programs accessible. For information, contact 214.768.4677.

NASHER SCULPTURE CE

The Nasher Sculpture Center will surely become a family favorite. Take time to marvel at the modern and contemporary sculptures in the two acre serene sculpture garden. The lush backdrop includes native trees and a tranquil fountain which bring down the temperature on even the hottest summer days.

The 55,000 square foot interior blends the beauty of the exterior well and gets you up close to 20th century paintings, drawings, and prints. Together the collection numbers more than 300 pieces with special exhibitions planned throughout the year.

Take advantage of the seasonal events for kids of all ages, including art scavenger hunts planned on the first Saturday per month when admission is free. Watch for additional free concerts and outdoor movies held throughout the year.

Additional Location Notes:
Nasher Café by Wolfgang Puck is open from 11am – 3:30pm.

The Nasher Store was voted "Best Museum Store" by D Magazine.

Downt
2001 Flora Street, Dallas 75201

214.242.5100

**nashersculpture
center.org**

Admission
Adults: $10
Seniors & Military: $7
Students with ID: $5
Children 12 and under: FREE!

FREE on the First Saturday per month with kids activities included.

Hours
Mondays: Closed
Tuesday – Sunday: 11am to 5pm

Holidays
Closed: Independence Day; Thanksgiving; Christmas Eve; Christmas Day; and New Year's Day

NATIONAL SCOUTING MUSEUM

Northwest / Irving
1329 W. Walnut Hill
Lane, Irving, 75038

972.580.2100

bsamuseum.org

Admission
Adults: $8
Senior: $6
Children 4 - 12: $6
Children 4 and under:
FREE

Admission is always
FREE on Sundays and
Mondays

Hours
Monday: 10am to 7pm
Tuesday – Saturday:
10am to 5pm
Sunday: 1pm to 5pm

The National Scouting Museum, located northwest of Dallas in Irving, was established in 1959. Take time to marvel at the 100+ year history of Scouting within the 53,000 square foot museum.

There are approximately 600,000 artifacts including paintings, uniforms, patches, photographs, film, and letters. There are 58 original Noman Rockwell paintings, including his World War I illustrations for *Red Cross Magazine.* The oldest artifact is a Chinese compass from 1500.

If your kids like nature and camping, they will surely enjoy the full-size replicas of campsites from 1910 and 1950.

OAK CLIFF CULTURAL CENTER

The relatively new Oak Cliff Cultural Center opened in 2010. The center includes an art gallery and multi-purpose studio.

Workshops, art, music, dance, summer camps, and cultural festivals are available for all ages. Exhibitions are usually focused on local artists and rotate every few months.

Southwest of Downtown / Oak Cliff
223 West Jefferson Blvd., Dallas 75208

214.670.3777

dallasculture.org/ oakcliffculturalcenter

Admission is FREE!
Some events have fees.

Hours
Tuesday – Friday:
3pm to 9pm
Saturday: 10am to 6pm

Oak Cliff

The neighborhood of Oak Cliff takes its name from the massive oak trees that line the street.

The Beaty, Leonard, and Coombes families settled in the area in 1837. The first permanent residence was built by William H. Hord in 1845. Almost 80 years later, Mr. and Mrs. Martin Weiss rescued this log cabin from demolition. It is now designated with an historic landmark and is located on Cockrell Hill Road at the American Legion Post.

It is estimated that more than one-million people have made Oak Cliff their home over the past one hundred years.

OLD RED MUSEUM
OF DALLAS COUNTY HISTORY & CULTURE

Downtown
100 South Houston
Street, Dallas 75202

214.745.1100

oldred.org

Admission
Adults: $8
Senior/student: $6
Children ages 3-16: $5
Children under 3:
FREE!

Early bird special on
Sundays: $5 for adults
if purchased before
noon

Group pricing
available (group-
sales@oldred.org /
214.757.1949)

Hours
Daily: 9am to 5pm

Holidays
Closed: Thanksgiving;
Christmas Eve' and
Christmas Day

Old Red has gone through many transformations over the years and is now the home to the Old Red Museum of Dallas County History and Culture. Original construction of the Old Red Courthouse took place in 1892 and when built it contained six courtrooms. The Romanesque revival-style building has been meticulously restored and includes many authentic features and architectural delights, including the 90 foot tall clock tower. The entire building serves as a testament of the craftsmanship of the time, including the fully restored Hatton W. Summers courtroom on the 4th floor.

The exhibits include a focus on Dallas' early years, the cities' transformation into a trading center, the "Big D" developments, and current culture. The Crystal Charity Ball Children's Education Center is a large hands-on education center designed specifically for younger visitors. The center includes over 40 touch screens that your kids will love. "Discovery carts" throughout the galleries highlight architecture, pioneer life, and Dallas facts.

Teachers: Consider renting "The Old Red Trunk" which comes with K-8 grade level appropriate learning tools on the judicial system, lesson plans, and extension possibilities. Two weeks rental runs about $35. Contact groupsales@oldred. org or 214.757.1949 for more information.

Additional Location Notes
Parking: $2 with museum admission.
DART: Short walk from West End or Union Station.

Museum shop, drinks and snacks, docent tours, and facility rental are available.

PEROT MUSEUM OF NATURE AND SCIE

"The museum reminds us that the universe is grander than ourselves, older than we can fathom, and that the world actually revolves around the sun, and not us." – Perot Museum website.

In 2008, the five Perot children donated $50 million for the new Victory Park location of the Museum of Nature to honor their parents, Margot and Ross Perot. By 2011, the rest of the $185 million fundraising goal was met and the museum opened in 2012 named in the Perot family's honor.

Standing about 14 stories high, the 180,000 square foot facility includes 11 permanent exhibit halls and 6 learning labs. Every inch of the building and outdoor space (including the roof top and outdoor play space) are geared towards stimulating curiosity.

When entering the main lobby, visitors are immediately in awe as they see the 35-foot Malawisaurus fossil. Continuing into the building, your family will see examples of engineering, sustainability, and technology working together. The Discovering Life Hall provides everything from single-cell organisms to complete ecosystems. You will be able to use brain waves to launch a ping-pong ball in the Being Human Hall and enjoy a challenge to introduce beneficial adaptations as you create a virtual animal in the T. Boone Pickens Life Then and Now Hall.

If you have children 5 or under, the Moody Family Children's Museum can't be missed. Expect to spend a considerable amount of time as there is just so much to discover. Your children will love to explore nature, dig for dinos,

Downtown
2201 N. Field Street,
Dallas 75201

214.428.5555

perotmuseum.org

General Exhibit Halls Admission:
Adults: $17
Senior: $12
Youth 2 - 17: $11
Educators, Members, and Children 2 and under are FREE!
Surcharges for the World's Largest Dinosaurs, Build It Garage Materials, and 3D films range from $2 to $8. Group rates and combo tickets are available. Tickets often sell out on weekends and holidays. Reserve tickets online.

Hours
Tickets are for timed entry at 30 minute intervals starting at 10am. Arrive early to ensure entry.
Monday – Saturday: 10am to 5pm
Sunday: Noon to 5pm
Extended hours the first Thursday of each month: open until 9pm

play in the art lab, and Discover Dallas through the mini Dallas Farmers Market and Dallas skyline.

Mark your calendar for the Second Saturday per month where the entire family can take part in Discovery Days (included in the cost of general admission). Also watch for the great events in The Lab on the first Thursday per month. Also included with general admission, you and your family will be able to interact with scientists, researchers, artists, and performers. You'll get to participate in experiments and design your own.

Don't forget to reserve a spot for the Story Time Under The Stars if you have children in the four to six range. Experience a delightful story, tutorial on the moon, stars, and constellations under the starry sky at the Portable Planetarium.

Early childhood programs (drop in and drop off), summer camps, sleep overs, field trips, birthday parties, and on-site classroom opportunities are available. Be sure to check the programs and events section on the website, it seems that the museum is adding delightful new activities daily. Catch them early and reserve your spot! This place is popular!

Additional Location Notes: Museum Parking Lot, under the Woodall Rodgers Freeway, available for $8, members pay $3. For handicap parking enter off Broom Street and attendants will direct to closest available spot.

Green Globes is a US green building guidance and assessment program. The Victory Park building secured the highest possible 4 Green Globes. Some of the green building and sustainability efforts:

- The building has a rainwater collection system that captures run-off water from the roof and parking lot, satisfying 74% of the museum's non-potable water needs and 100% of its irrigation needs
- The gardens use drip irrigation which is 75% more effective than sprinklers
- The buildings cube shape is more energy efficient than a traditional rectangle building design
- The furniture is made from wood taken from sustainable forests
- The building also features LED lighting, off-grid energy generation technology, and solar-powered water heating

PEROT MUSEUM OF NATURE AND SCIENCE AT FAIR PARK

The Dallas Museum of Natural History was built as part of the 1936 Texas Centennial Exhibition in Fair Park.

In 2012, the museum converted to a second campus for the Perot Museum. It features exhibits such as Mineral Majesty, Light Play, and historical dioramas.

East / Fair Park
3535 Grand Ave.
Dallas 75210

perotmuseum.org

Fair Park information:
fairpark.org

Admission
Adults: $1
Free for members

Admission to the Fair Park campus is included with your Perot Museum visit if ticket is presented at the Fair Park box office.

Hours
Friday – Sunday:
Noon to 5pm

SIXTH FLOOR MUSEUM AT DEALEY PLAZA

Downtown
411 Elm at Houston
Dallas 75202

214.747.6660

jfk.org

Admission
Adults: $16
Senior: $14
Children 6-18: $13
Children 5 and under:
FREE!

Hours
Monday: Noon to 6pm
Tuesday – Sunday:
10am to 6pm

Holidays
Closed: Thanksgiving
and Christmas

**Additional Location
Notes**
DART: Union Station
and West End Station

Parking: Adjacent to
museum is $5

Wheelchair Accessible and strollers are
welcome. An accessible
entrance is located on
the northwest corner of
the museum.

The Sixth Floor Museum chronicles the November 22, 1963 assassination of President John F. Kennedy. The museum is located on the sixth and seventh floors of the warehouse formerly known as the Texas School Book Depository, a large red brick building in the West End Historic District of downtown.

The sixth floor includes a permanent exhibit of photographs, films, and artifacts that chronicle President Kennedy's life, death, and legacy. You will also visit the sniper's perch and storage space where a rifle was found.

The seventh floor is home to visiting exhibits. A Reading Room also overlooks Dealey Plaza and includes an extensive library of books, magazines, newspapers, and media. For Reading Room entry, send requests to readingroom@jfk.org.

Tickets are by timed entry in 30 minute increments. As such, some entry times may sell out and it is recommended to buy tickets in advance online. Plan about 90 minutes for your visit. Audio guides are provided with the cost of admission.

Family CSI Days are planned regularly with mock crime scenes, police reports, and forensic evidence stations. Group visit options are available. Contact 214.747.6660 or e-mail groupsales@jfk.org for more information. Museum Store + Café are located across the street and operated locally.

Teachers! Educator's Guide is available online. In addition, the museum hosts teacher training sessions.

When visiting the museum, be sure to visit the Kennedy Memorial Plaza which is located one block east of Dealey Plaza between Main and Commerce Streets. On June 25, 1970, the aesthetically simple monument was dedicated as a place of reflection and remembrance. Each year on the anniversary of President Kennedy's assassination, hundreds gather in the plaza to pay respects.

The Texas School Book Depository

The Texas School Book Depository was constructed in 1901. When the Texas School Book Depository moved out in 1970 some hoped the building would be torn down as it served as a reminder of President Kennedy's assassination in 1963.

Luckily, the building remained and was restored by Dallas County after the 1977 acquisition. On President's Day 1989, the Sixth Floor Museum opened in response to fill the need of visitors who came to Dealey Plaza to learn more about the assassination. Thirteen years later and again on President's Day, the museum expanded to the seventh floor.

SOUTH DALLAS CULTURAL CENTER

East / Fair Park
Just outside of Fair
Park at the Southern
Gate
3400 South Fitzhugh,
Dallas 75210

214.939.2787

**dallasculture.org/
SDCulturalCenter**

Admission is FREE!
Possible fees for special
events.

Hours
Sunday & Monday:
Closed
Tuesday, Thursday,
and Friday:
1pm to 9pm
Wednesday and
Saturday:
9am to 5pm

Created in 1982 and renovated in 2007, the South Dallas Cultural Center provides a multi-purpose art facility across from Fair Park. The center includes a 120-seat theater, a visual arts gallery, and studios for dance, printmaking, and photography. The center also has a digital recording studio.

The center offers creative and educational activities for children. The Soul Children's Theater provides family-oriented theater and educational programs aimed at creating an understanding and appreciation of African diaspora. A summer arts camp and fall/spring classes are available.

TEXAS SCULPTURE GARDEN

Located inside and just outside of the lobby of the Texas at Hall Office Park, the Texas Sculpture Garden celebrates the work of many prominent Texas artists. In addition to the sculptures, the outdoor area includes winding walking trails, lush landscape, lakes and fountains.

Far North / Frisco
6801 Gaylord Parkway, Frisco 75034

texassculpture garden.org

Admission: FREE!

Hours
Monday - Friday:
9am to 5pm
Saturday: 9am to Noon

Outside artwork:
Open dawn to dusk

Are We There Yet? Dallas

Film, Theatre, and
the Sound of Music

This chapter is dedicated to performances, both theatrical and musical. Some of the entries are based on specific companies and others are based on venues. The venues listed were narrowed down to locations that are most likely to attract a family audience. Most of the companies listed provide opportunities for classes, camps, or workshops. Times, admission, or class cost will vary based on the program.

Denton Arthur Coley is famous for performing the first implantation of a total artificial heart. He is founder and surgeon in chief of the Texas Heart Institute. In the late 60s and early 70s, he played upright bass in a swing band called the "Heart Beats".

THE BLACK ACADEMY OF ARTS AND LETTERS (TBAAL)

Downtown
Dallas Convention
Center Theatre
Complex
1309 Canton Street,
Dallas 75202

214.743.2400

tbaal.org

Started in 1977, The Black Academy of Arts and Letters (TBAAL) is dedicated to creating and enhancing awareness of art and culture utilizing the framework of African, African-American, and Caribbean Arts and Letters.

Located in downtown Dallas and housed in the Dallas Convention Center Theatre Complex, it is the nation's only arts institution and African American organization housed in a major urban convention center. Annually, TBAAL presents over 100 programs in theatre, music, dance, literary arts, film, and visual arts. In addition, TBAAL provides summer programs and workshops for kids.

CARA MIA THEATER COMPANY

West of Oak Lawn
3630 Harry Hines Blvd.
#3b, Dallas 75219

214.516.0706

caramiatheatre.org

The Cara Mia Theater Company was started in 1996 and quickly filled the void for a theater that focuses on the Mexican-American experience. Using theater, literature, and education programs, the non-profit company broadens the understanding of Chicano and Latino culture.

In conjunction with the Oak Cliff Cultural Center and the Big Thought's Thriving Minds, the School of YES Summer Camp is provided for children ages 7-14. The students participate in theatre, dance, music, and visual arts with an end of the camp performance.

CHILDREN'S CHORUS OF GREATER DALLAS

Children's Chorus of Greater Dallas (CCGD) is the official children's chorus of the Dallas Symphony Orchestra. The 550 children and teens in grades 4-12 make CCGD one of the largest and most prestigious youth choral programs in America.

The programs include a Summer Singing Camp, Downtown Chorus, Neighborhood Chorus, and Outreach Chorus. Check the website to learn more about program registration and upcoming performances.

Performances throughout town
400 North St. Paul Street, Suite 510, Dallas 75201

214.965.0491

thechildrens chorus.org

DALLAS ANGELIKA FILM CENTER CRYBABY MATINÉE

The eight screen Angelica Film Center is located in the heart of Mockingbird Station and is dedicated to showing quality independent films.

The Crybaby Matinee is available every Tuesday and Wednesday. Enjoy and relax without the worry of disturbing the audience. Café is available.

Mockingbird Station
5321 E. Mockingbird Lane, Dallas 75206

214.841.4713

angelikafilm center.com

DALLAS BLACK DANCE THEATRE

Downtown
2700 Ann Williams
Way, Dallas 75201

214.871.2376

dbdt.com

The Dallas Black Theater is the oldest, continuously operating professional dance company in Dallas. The company consists of 12 professional, full-time dancers performing a mixed repertory. Watch the events calendar for the performance schedule. Be sure to keep an eye out for the student matinées available throughout the season with ticket costs at $5.

The Dallas Black Dance Academy, established in 1974, is the official school of the Dallas Black Dance Theatre. The Academy offers a wide range of classes in ballet, jazz, African, modern, hip-hop, and tap. Regular classes are offered September through May.

DALLAS CHILDREN'S THEATER

Northeast
5938 Skillman,
Dallas 75231

214.740.0051

dct.org

The Dallas Children's Theater (DCT) always has an amazing line up of performances with classic storybooks brought to life on stage, holiday favorites, and special area premieres. Performances often include after the show options with activities, treats, games, and giveaways. Watch the performance listing for options and age recommendations.

DCT also offers a variety of theater and video classes designed by age/grade level. Most classes offer a performance at the end of the season. Volunteer opportunities are available for ages 13+.

Teachers! Be sure to check out the Student Matinée Performance Series and plan an awesome field trip.

106

THE DALLAS OPERA

The Dallas Opera offers student performance programs, including an excellent introduction to opera with Bastien and Bastienne (one of Mozart's earliest works which was written when he was 12). Student Matinées are also available with an excellent price of $4 per ticket. Dress Rehearsals are also a great opportunity to introduce your 6th graders and up to the opera and are FREE.

The FREE Kids Opera Boot Camps provides 3 hour workshops with hands-on activities that teach what it takes to put on an opera. The class concludes with a fully-staged performance.

Downtown
Margot and Bill Winspear Opera House, 2403 Flora Street, Suite 500, Dallas 75201

214.443.1042

dallasopera.org

DALLAS PUPPET THEATER

Check the performance calendar for show times and venues or book your own event geared towards ages 3-10.

puppetry.org

DALLAS SUMMER MUSICALS (DSM)

**dallassummer
musicals.org**

In 2015, Dallas Summer Musicals (DSM) will celebrate its 75th anniversary. Over the years, DSM has provided continued dedication to bringing quality musical theatre and Broadway shows to the Southwest region. Dallas Summer Musicals (DSM) produces and presents year-round at various venues throughout North Texas. Show times are available on the website and many performances are geared toward a younger audience.

Classes and workshops in singing, acting, dancing are available through the DSM Academy of Performing Arts. The DSM Kids Club is free to join and provides lots of fun activities and invitations to club events.

DALLAS SYMPHONY ORCHESTRA (DSO)

Encourage the love of music by taking your children to one of the special Dallas Symphony Orchestra (DSO) family concerts, such as the Halloween Organ Spooktacular. Watch the Dallas Symphony Orchestra (DSO) calendar of events for options at the Meyerson Symphony Center, community concerts (DSO on the GO), and outreach programs. DSO offers season or single tickets and some community concerts are free to the public.

Another great family offering is the educational programs for grades K-12. Each youth concert is designed with a specific age group in mind and will provide equal amounts of entertainment and education. Reservations are made by completing and mailing in the Youth Concert reservation form. Tickets are $6.50 (adult or child).

Be sure to check out DSOKids.com. One of the great offerings is the instrument encyclopedia which lets your kids hear what every instrument in the orchestra sounds like. You'll also be able to learn more about youth concerts, youth programs, open rehearsals, and much more.

Downtown
Meyerson Symphony Center
2301 Flora Street, Dallas 75201

214.692.0203

mydso.com

dsokids.com

Additional Location Notes:
DART: Red, Blue, and Green lines to Pearl and Bryan Streets
Parking: $10 at the Hall Arts Center Garage on Ross Avenue

You may also want to join the DSO Kids Club. Membership includes special DSO trinkets, discounts, and your child may even get a chance to go back stage and meet the musicians!

For teen musicians and music lovers, check out studiodso.com to ask musicians questions, post your own concert reviews, see video master classes, and more.

For African American and Latino string players, the Young Strings Program is available. It is designed to increase multicultural diversity in American orchestras and auditions are held each January. Those accepted will receive mentoring, performance opportunities, instruction, concert tickets, and more.

109

DALLAS WINDS

Downtown
Meyerson Symphony
Center
2301 Flora Street
Dallas 75201

214.565.9463

dws.org

The Dallas Wind Symphony, renamed Dallas Winds in 2014, is a 50 plus civilian wind band that performs at the Meyerson Concert Center. Also watch for community shows and summer outdoor concerts.

Dallas Winds Band Camp offers instruction and performance opportunities to band students from the Dallas Independent School District.

Also watch for dates for the Backstage Classes that take children behind the curtain to learn about the instruments and meet the musicians.

FINE ARTS CHAMBER PLAYERS (FACP)

**Design District /
NW of Downtown**
Sammons Center for
the Arts, 3630 Harry
Hines Blvd., Suite 302,
Dallas 75219

214.520.2219

**fineartschamber
players.org**

Founded in 1981, the Fine Arts Chamber Players (FACP) provides FREE concerts of classical music. Most concerts are performed at the Horchow Auditorium in the Dallas Museum of Art located in the Dallas Arts District (1717 N. Harwood Street, Dallas, TX 75201).

FACP also offers an abundance of FREE educational programs taught by professional teaching artists. The Dream Collectors, Music A-Z, Masterclasses,

and Music Residencies provide short and long term professional instruction for grades K-12.

The Fine Arts Chamber Players also run Project Workbench which locates instruments, repairs them, and places them with students and schools at no charge. Basically, they are awesome and if you are looking for a non-profit to support in Dallas, I highly recommend them. Donations can be made online.

GALAXY DRIVE-IN

Return to the nostalgic days of the drive-in with two showings per night. Six screens to choose from. No outside drinks or food are allowed. Snack bar opens at 6pm with reasonable prices. Mini-golf available with kids 3 and under free.

Southeast / Ennis
5301 N Interstate
Highway 45
Ennis 75119

972.875.5505

**galaxydrivein
theatre.com**

Admission
Adults: $7
Children 11 and under:
$3

**Open 7 nights a week,
365 nights a year.**

KATHY BURKS THEATRE OF PUPPETRY ARTS

Kathy Burks Theatre of Pupperty Arts annually presents two original puppet plays as part of the Dallas Children's Theater (DCT) Main Stage season. Katy Burks Puppet Theater also collaborates with DCT when puppets are needed for their performances, such as The Velveteen Rabbit.

The Rosewood Center houses the Kathy Burks' antique collection, including Sue Hastings' marionettes and extremely rare 1930's Disney marionettes.

Northeast
Rosewood Center for
Family Arts
5938 Skillman
Dallas 75231

214.587.7543

**kathyburks
puppets.com**

MAJESTIC THEATRE

Downtown
1925 Elm Street,
Dallas, 75201

214.670.3687

**dallasculture.org/
majestictheatre**

Located in the heart of Downtown at the corner of Elm and Harwood, the Majestic Theatre opened on April 21, 1921 as a vaudeville theatre. By the 1930s, the theatre started to present movies with big stars in attendance.

The last movie was shown in 1973. It reopened after a major restoration in 1983. It is now a performing arts venue managed by the City of Dallas Office of Cultural Affairs.

METROPOLITAN WINDS

P.O. Box 670925
Dallas 75367

972.680.4444

**metropolitan
winds.org**

The members of the Metropolitan Winds ensemble are professional musicians, band directors, and private music teachers. They often perform at the Dallas City Performance Hall in the Dallas Arts District (2520 Flora Street). Tickets generally run $35, but you should also watch the concert schedule for free performances especially around the holidays in local malls or churches.

MEADOWS SCHOOL OF THE ARTS

Meadows provides a robust Performing Arts Season, including student performances. Dates and times are available online.

The Meadows Ticket Office is in the lobby of the Greer Garson Theatre. Tickets can also be purchased one hour prior to the performance at the Bob Hope Theatre or Caruth Auditorium.

University Park
6101 Bishop,
Dallas 75275

214.768.2000

smu.edu/Meadows

MORTON H. MEYERSON SYMPHONY CENTER

The Meyerson Symphony Center is owned and operated by the City of Dallas Office of Cultural Affairs. The primary tenant is the Dallas Symphony Orchestra (DSO), but many others perform in the concert hall. On an annual basis there are over 325 performances.

DART: Red, Blue, and Green lines to Pearl and Bryan Streets

Parking: $10 at the Hall Arts Center Garage on Ross Avenue. Valet parking at the Flora Street main entrance.

Downtown
2301 Flora Street,
Dallas 75201

214.670.3600

**dallasculture.org/
meyerson
symphonycenter**

MUSIC HALL AT FAIR PARK

East / Fair Park
909 First Avenue,
Dallas 75210

214.565.1116

**liveatthemusic
hall.com**

DART: Green line
to Buckner Station.
Parking: Fair Park
grounds or lots on First
and Second Avenue.
Fees for parking vary
by event. Use Perry
Street entrance for
wheelchair access.

The Music Hall at Fair Park had its
theatrical debut on October 10, 1925
with the musical premiere of Sigmund
Romberg's *The Student Prince*.

Since then, the hall has continued to
provide a venue for Broadway musical
touring companies, grand opera, ballet,
pageants, and public functions.

Lucky for us the renovations to the
Spanish Baroque style hall have
been functional improvements (air
conditioning, back stage enlargements,
and seating improvements). The Art
Deco elegance has been preserved.

Check events schedule to plan your
family visit.

SHAKESPEARE DALLAS

Downtown
Samuell Grand Park,
1500 Tension Parkway,
Dallas 75223

East
The Bath House
Cultural Center,
521 East Lawther
Drive, Dallas 75218

North
Addison Circle Park,
4970 Addison Circle,
Addison 75001

214.559.2778

shakespearedallas.org

The core program, Shakespeare in the
Park, started in 1971 with a one-man
version of Hamlet. In 1984, the company
introduced Shakespeare on the Go! the
in-school program for grades 3-12.

By 2001, the company started the
transition to year-round events and
expanded the venue offerings to include
the Addison Circle Park and The Bath
House Cultural Center.

114

POCKET SANDWICH THEATRE

Started in 1980, the Pocket Sandwich Theatre, focuses of performances of unabashedly "entertainment" theatre – mainly comedies and melodramas. The Pocket Theatre provides a friendly, casual atmosphere. Food and dinner service is optional. Popcorn throwing at the actors is welcomed.

Mockingbird Central Plaza
5400 East Mockingbird Lane, Dallas 75206

214.821.1860

pocketsandwich.com

Admission
Thursday: $12
Friday: $20
Saturday: $25
Sunday: $15
Seniors and Children 12 and under are $2 off

TEXAS BALLET

Be sure to check for the dates to see a free performance of the Nutcracker or Peter and the Wolfe. In addition, performances are available throughout the year at various performance halls in Dallas and Fort Worth.

The Texas Ballet Theater also offers summer programs and weekend/ weeknight classes focusing on modern, tap, ballet, and contemporary dance.

Dallas School
670 North Coit Road, Suite 2379, Richardson 75080

214.377.8576

texasballettheater.org

Are We There Yet? Dallas

Animals All Around

THE CHILDREN'S AQUARIUM AT FAIR PARK

East / Fair Park
1462 First Avenue,
Dallas 75210

469.554.7340

**childrensaquarium-
fairpark.com**

Admission:
Adults: $8
Senior: $6
Children 3 - 11: $6
Children 2 and under:
FREE!

Hours
7 days a week:
9am to 4:30pm

Holidays
Closed: Thanksgiving
and Christmas

**Additional Location
Notes:**
Parking: Free at Fair
Park (except during the
State Fair of Texas)

DART: Green Line to
Fair Park Station

Wheelchair
accessible and strollers
are welcome

The Children's Aquarium at Fair Park is the perfect adventure on a hot summer day and by far one of the best for the preK set. The exhibits are at the right eye level for the little ones and there are opportunities to touch and feed fish. The small venue size is a plus for this age group as well; your family can visit the entire facility without overextending a tot's energy or interest.

One downfall...lots of other people feel the same way and it can get a bit crowded. Planning a trip earlier in the day or during the week will help ensure you get the best views. However, you may want to take advantage of the 2:30 pm daily fish feeding demonstration.

The aquarium has two small inside wings that highlight freshwater, intertidal, shore, and near shore. Outside at Stingray Bay, you will have the opportunity to pet and feed stingray and watch the big tank for the cow nose ray and zebra and bonnet head sharks.

Watch for Homeschool Day with discounted entry and educational activities for K- 5th grade. Pre-registration is required and the space is limited.

Half and full day camps are available for children age 3 through grade 5. The camps for older children often split the day with activities at the Texas Discovery Gardens, also located in Fair Park.

Want to sleep with the fish? Overnight stay is available for $40/participant. Participants must be at least 7 years old and will get to experience crafts, a guided evening tour, a nighttime snack, and breakfast. Check the website for available nights, chaperone requirements, and booking instructions.

Party room is available for up to 25 guests. Birthday party package are available on Saturdays and Sundays. The fee includes room, an animal encounter, complimentary stingray feeding, and tableware.

Annual passes are available and Dallas Zoo Memberships provide discounted admission rates.

Albino Alligators

The Children's Aquarium at Fair Park is home to an Albino American Alligator.

There are fewer than 50 Albino American Alligators living in the United States.

The albino alligator lacks or has an inhibited gene for melanin, the brown pigment for the skin and eye's iris.

Due to the lack of melanin, the albino's eyes look red because the underlying blood vessels in the iris can be seen.

DALLAS WORLD AQUARIUM (DWA)

Downtown
1801 North Griffin St.,
Dallas 75202

214.720.2224

dwazoo.com

Admission:
Adults: $20.95
Senior: $16.95
Children 2 - 12: $14.95
Children 1 and under:
FREE

Take public transportation and get $1 off regular admission

Military admission discounts (photo ID required)

Hours
Daily: 9am to 5pm

Holidays
Closed: Thanksgiving and Christmas

Additional Location Notes:
Parking: Downtown lots for $3-$8

DART: West End Station

Wheelchair Accessible and strollers are welcome and available for rent

The Dallas World Aquarium (DWA) is located downtown in two buildings built in the early 1920s. The interiors were completely demolished, leaving only the brick walls and support structure. The alley between both buildings became a channel between the freshwater and saltwater ecosystems on display.

In 2002, ten years after opening, DWA added another area, the Mundo Maya, in a newly constructed building. Mundo Maya is the crown of DWA with the 400,000-gallon walk-through exhibit with sharks, rays, and sea turtles of the Yucatan Peninsula.

DWA also includes Orinco, a seven-story exhibit that highlights the South American rainforest ecosystem. The Borneo features Australasian birds, fish, and mammals.

Outdoors, there is a year round South African exhibit with close up views of black-footed penguins and storks. There is also a traditional aquarium gallery which features coral reef and kelp forest ecosystems.

Feeding schedule starts at 10:30 with the otters and ends with the sharks at 4:30. Visit the website to see the full feeding schedule with opportunities every half hour.

Paedomorphism

Paedomorphism, also known as neoteny, is the retention of juvenile or larval traits into adulthood.

At DWA, you can see an example of neoteny in the axolotl, a Mexican relative to the tiger salamander. Axolotl, also know as the "Mexican walking fish", is actually an amphibian that reaches adulthood without undergoing metamorphosis and keeps their external gills throughout life.

The axolotl is only native to Lake Xochimilco and Lake Chalco in central Mexico. Wild axolotls are near extinction due to pollution and the urbanization of Mexico City. A large number are bred in captivity for pets and research.

DALLAS ZOO

South of Downtown
650 South R.L. Thornton Freeway (I-35E take Marsalis exit), Dallas 75203

469.554.7500

dallaszoo.com

Admission:
Adults: $15
Senior: $12 ($5 admission on Wednesdays)
Children 3 - 11: $12
Children 2 and under: FREE

Mon. - Tues.
Ride DART and get a $2 discount

Admission prices drop to $5 in January and February

Watch the website or join the mailing list for specials, such as $1 admission days

Hours
Daily: 9am to 5pm

Holidays
Closed on Christmas

Additional Location Notes:
Parking: $8
DART: Red Line to the Dallas Zoo Station

The Dallas Zoo dates from 1888 when the city of Dallas purchased two deer and two mountain lions from a man in Colorado City for $60. It was originally located in City Park (currently Dallas Heritage Village) and moved to Fair Park in 1910. By 1912, the zoo moved again to Marsalis Park in Oak Cliff.

Through numerous community campaigns and with help from the Federal Works Projects Administration (WPA), the zoo continued to grow and was named one of the 10 largest zoos in the country by 1940.

Through the remainder of the 1900s, the zoo continued to develop, including more focus on research and conservation. In the early 2000s, the Zoo had some rough years, including a gorilla escape in 2004.

By 2009, the city of Dallas turned over management of the zoo to private management and by 2010 the completion of the Giants of the Savanna exhibit brought new community confidence.

And indeed there should be confidence in the Dallas Zoo as it has earned numerous accolades, including being listed in the Nation's Top 10 Zoos by USA Today and having the best African zoo exhibit by Zoobook. Today, the Dallas Zoo features a 106-acre park, thousands of animals, and an education department that offers programs for all ages.

A 67½-foot-tall giraffe (and tallest statue in Texas) greets you at the entrance, preparing you for the unique experience you will have when visiting the Giants of Savanna exhibit.

> The St. Louis artist Bob James Cassilly and his team created the 67½-foot-tall giraffe at the entrance of the zoo. Although the giraffe is the tallest statue he ever made, he is well known for other large works and ideas, including a 50-foot squid at the St. Louis Zoo, Hippo Sculptures at Central Park's Safari Playground, and a series of 25 to 40-foot turtles at Turtle Park in St. Louis
>
> Cassilly also helped create the City Museum in downtown St. Louis. The museum includes an aquarium, shoelace factory, a fire truck, airplanes, and a ferris wheel on the roof. The interesting mix, artistic style, and imagination helped put it on the PBS list of "The Great Public Places in the World".

Unlike many zoos where you see giraffes at a distance, you are eye to eye with these beautiful animals in Dallas. The Wilds of Africa exhibit is an 11-acre African savanna and includes every major habitat of the continent. The Monorail Safari is available to take guests on a one-mile tour through six habitats and many of the animals in the Wilds can only be seen by monorail.

The Lacerte Family Children's Zoo includes ponies for riding and birds to feed. There are educational and interactive exhibits for kids of all ages.

Looking for food? Skip the Zoofari Food Court and the Wilds of Africa Grill. Head to the Serengeti Grill that has floor-to-ceiling observation windows; often with a lion lazing right against the glass.

There is a great variety of camp options, early childhood programs, and homeschool opportunities. The zoo also offers sleepovers and family camp outs. Safari night hikes are also held on select Fridays and Saturdays.

Not into the night life, try the Backstage Safari program for a 90 minute guided tour that includes feeding elephants, holding penguins, and experiencing a special show. Make your registrations early. (Minimum age is 5; cost is $89-$99 for adults and $69-$79 for youth).

Check out the citizen science based club, the Frog Club, for children 8 and up. Frog Clubbers receive special Texas Parks and Wildlife Amphibian training and can participate with Dallas Zoo staff to record the native frog species that live at River Legacy Park in Arlington, TX. Frog Club meetings are held approximately once per month from April through August.

THE GENTLE ZOO

Far East / Forney, TX
(About 25 minutes East
of Downtown Dallas)
12600 FM 2932,
Forney 75126

469.834.2857

gentlezoo.com

Admission:
Adults: $5
Senior: $5
Children 1 and under:
FREE

Hours
Monday: Closed
Tuesday – Friday:
9:30am to 2pm
Saturday:
9:30am to 5pm
Sunday: 11am to 5pm

The Gentle Zoo offers a petting zoo, indoor party rooms, playground, train rides, and picnic areas. Party packages are available.

Best times to visit include when the Gentle Zoo has additional special events. In spring, visit for the excellent Easter celebrations and Easter egg hunts. In fall, be sure to join in on the fun to be had at the Pumpkin Patch.

HEARD NATURAL SCIENCE MUSEUM AND WILDLIFE SANCTUARY

Most of the Heard is preserved or restored to the natural ecosystem allowing for excellent nature walks. Animal talks and guided trails are available.

Two nature gardens and also available to learn about wildlife friendly landscapes, wildlife habitats, native plants, and residential birds and butterflies.

The indoor exhibits highlight various aspects of the North Texas ecosystem and provides a fossil dig and a marine room. The Heard also includes an extensive selection of natural science items, including minerals, rocks, sea shells, insets, and mammal skins.

The Animals of the World exhibit provides a home to non-releasable and non-native animals including macaws, capybara, mongoose, lemurs, deer, and more.

Children will enjoy the pioneer village with eight play school scale structures that would have been typical in a 1800s prairie settlement.

Mark your calendar for the Third Saturday Nature Talks that start at 9:30 and are included with general admission. Each nature talk focuses on native plants or animals and provides an excellent opportunity to learn more. Preregistration is required as space is limited.

Nature Store, summer camps, birthday parties, and facility rentals are available.

Far North / McKinney
1 Nature Place,
McKinney 75069

972.562.5566

heardmuseum.org

Admission
(prices vary by season)
Adults: $9 - $11
Senior: $6 - $8
Children 3 - 12: $6 - $8
Members and children
2 and under are FREE!

Hours
Monday: Closed
Tuesday – Saturday:
9am to 5pm
Sunday: 1 to 5pm

The Heard stays open until 7:30 on the second Saturday of every month.

Holidays
Closed: Thanksgiving, Christmas, and New Year's Day
Open until 3pm on Christmas Eve and New Year's Eve

SEA LIFE GRAPEVINE AQUARIUM

**Far Northwest /
Grapevine**
(Grapevine Mills Mall)
3000 Grapevine Mills
Mall, Grapevine 76051

877.819.7677

**visitsealife.com/
grapevine**

Admission
Adults: $20
Children 3 - 12: $16
Children 2 and under:
FREE

Hours
Monday – Friday:
10am to 6:30pm
Saturday:
10am to 7:30pm
Sunday:
11am to 5:30pm

Sea Life is a two-story 45,000 square-foot indoor aquarium. Get up close with sharks, sea turtles, stingrays, sea horses, jellyfish and more. Feeding times can be viewed online.

Get wet at the Interactive Rockpool where your children can touch a sea star, crab, sea urchin, shark pup, or horseshoe crab. Get wild in the submarine play zone. Then, relax at the Dive Discovery Cinema.

Birthday parties are available.

Book online to save up to 25%.

Bring 20 plastic grocery bags to your next visit and receive a 10% discount on standard door admission.

TEXAS DISCOVERY GARDENS IN FAIR PARK

The Texas Discovery Gardens is a 7.5 acre, 100% organic botanical collection featuring native plants and select species from other regions. All plants are selected based on the habitat benefits they provide for native wildlife, including butterflies, bugs, and birds.

There are ten themed areas including a butterfly habitat, native wildlife point, scent garden, share garden, and heirloom garden.

Inside the two-story Rosine Smith Sammons Butterfly House and Insectarium, you can enjoy the feel of a tropical rain forest, complete with hundreds of free-flying butterflies, more than 60 species of tropical plants, and rotating insect and arthropod displays. Be sure to visit at noon, when the daily release of newly-emerged butterflies is held in the Butterfly House.

The garden hosts guided tours, gardening workshops, plant sales, and family events throughout the year. Of special note, mark your calendar for the annual festivals: Fangs in June; Butterflies and Bugs in August; and the Creepy Crawl-o-ween Day in October.

Butterfly and Rainforest themed birthday party packages are available. A wide variety of educational classes are available for both adults and children (some with additional costs). Day camps are also available for children 3 years old through 5th grade.

East / Fair Park
(Gate 6 in Fair Park)
3601 Martin Luther King Jr Blvd,
Dallas 75210

214.428.7476 ext. 341

texasdiscover gardens.org

Admission
Adults: $8
Senior: $6
Children 3 - 11: $4
Children 3 and under: FREE

Each Tuesday, the gardens are open for FREE (butterfly house is regular admission). Also, watch the website for FREE admission days

Hours
Daily: 10am to 5pm

Holidays
Closed: New Year's Day, Thanksgiving Day, and Christmas Eve and Day

Are We There Yet? Dallas

Take it Outside
(Parks and Recreation)

ABBOTT PARK

Highland Park
4814 Abbott Avenue,
Dallas 75219

**tx-highlandpark.
civicplus.com**

Abbott Park provides a great animal themed playground. Although this park does not have restrooms, I cannot say enough for any Dallas playground that offers shade.

ADDISON CIRCLE PARK

North / Addison
4950 Addison Circle
Drive, Addison 75001

addisontx.gov

This ten acre open space serves as the main special events site in Addison. It also provides a great water feature which your kids will greatly appreciate in the heat of the Dallas summer.

BACHMAN LAKE / BACHMAN LAKE TRAIL

Bachman Lake is a 205 acre freshwater lake near Love Field. It was originally built in 1903 as a water source for Dallas, but was soon found too small for the needs and was replaced by White Rock Lake by 1911.

There is a 3.5 mile trail surrounding the lake with periodic benches and water fountains. There is a restroom on the south side. Due to the proximity to Love Field, the trail can be a bit noisy, but fun for children who are still at the age to be amazed by planes.

Northwest / Love Field
3500 Northwest Highway, Dallas 75201

dallascounty.org

Parking:
Shorecrest Drive,
Lakefield Boulevard,
and Bachman Drive.

DART: Bachman
Station

BECKERT PARK

Located between Quorum Drive and the North Dallas Tollway, Beckert Park is surrounded by the high rises of North Dallas. The park is energetic and features an outdoor summer series with jazz, salsa, and symphony.

North / Addison
5044 Addison Circle
Drive, Addison 75001

972.450.2851

addisontx.gov

BOB JONES NATURE CENTER AND PRESERVE

**Far Northwest /
Southlake, TX**
(Southwest of Dallas /
Past DFW and Grape-
vine on Grapevine
Lake)
355 E. Bob Jones Rd.,
Southlake 76092

817.491.6333

bjnc.org

Admission is FREE!

Hours
Nature Center
Monday: Closed
Tuesday – Saturday:
9am to 5pm

Preserve and Trails
Daily: 7am to 5pm;
7am to 8pm during
daylight savings time

In 2008, the Bob Jones Nature Center and Preserve opened as an educational center that includes 76 acres on the Preserve with access to almost 400 acres of Cross Timbers habitat.

There are also 20 miles of trails on the Walnut Grove National Recreation Trail which pass through forest and pocket prairies on Lake Grapevine. Trail maps are available online or in the nature center. Dogs are not permitted.

The Cross Timbers ecosystem includes post oak, blackjack oak, eastern red cedar, black oak, ash, and black hickory trees. The area is a sanctuary for foxes, coyotes, bobcats, wild turkey, and white-tailed deer. Many migratory birds, waterfowl, and birds of prey pass through or stop for the winter.

Classes, camps, and workshops are available for all ages. There are also many options for Girl and Boy Scout programs. Themed birthday parties are available through the nature center.

Consider signing up for Membership to support the Center and receive great discounts.

*The preserve and nature center are named after John Dolford "Bob" Jones. Bob was a slave working on his father's farm in Roanoke, Texas. After the Civil War, he was set free and he, his mother, and brother bought a 60-acre farm in Southlake.
As Bob's family grew, so did the farm – eventually expanding to 2,000 acres. In the 1990s, some of the remaining land belonging to the Jones farm was purchased by Southlake and developed into the Bob Jones Nature Center and Preserve.*

BOB WOODRUFF PARK

Big trees and a relaxing setting are in store for your family when you visit Bob Woodruff Park in Plano. The park features hard surface trails, sand volleyball courts, restrooms, and a playground for all ages.

North / Plano
2601 San Gabriel Drive,
Plano 75074

972.941.7250

plano.gov

CAMPION TRAILS

The Campion Trail is Irving's initiative to develop a greenbelt trail that connects with the regional trail system and links the cities within the Metroplex. See the website for trail maps, a brief description of each trail, and access locations with parking.

West / Irving

**cityofirving.org/
parks-and-recreation/
trail-information.asp**

CEDAR HILL STATE PARK & JOE POOL LAKE

**Southwest /
Cedar Hill**
1570 F.M. 1382,
Cedar Hill 75104

972.291.3900

cedarhillstatepark.org

Admission:
Adults/Seniors:
Day Use $ 7
Overnight $5
Senior:
Children 12 and under:
FREE

The 1,826 acre park and 7,500 acre Joe Pool Lake can make you feel like you have really left the city; yet the drive to Cedar Hill is actually quite quick.

There are biking and hiking trails, a swimming beach, picnic tables and grilles, and fishing. There are also over 300 campsites, so plan to stay overnight.

In addition to selling bait, the Joe Pool Marina rents ski boats, jet skis, pontoon boats, and paddle boats. Call 972.299.9010 for pricing and availability.

Live Adventure, located next to the swimming beach, rents kayaks and mountain bikes.

CEDAR RIDGE PRESERVE

Far Southwest
7171 Mountain Creek
Parkway, Dallas 75249

972.709.7784

**audubondallas.org/
cedarridge.html**

Admission is FREE!

Hours
Monday: Closed
Tuesday – Sunday:
November – March
6:30am to 6pm
April – October
6:30am to 8:30pm

Cedar Ridge Preserve is managed by Audubon Dallas and is a natural habitat of 600 acres with 9 miles of trails lined with native trees and grasses. Along the trails, you will find butterfly gardens and limited picnic areas. A trail map is available for download from the website.

Family days, craft events, and camp outs for the family are held throughout the year. Check the dates and prices on the website.

Consider putting the family to work on the trail or in the butterfly gardens. The third Saturday of each month is Habitat Restoration and Trail Maintenance time. Tools, snacks, and water are provided. Contact info_CRP@yahoo.com for more information.

CELEBRATION PARK

Celebration Park is located at Malone Drive and Angel Parkway in Allen. It offers 104 acres of outdoor recreation, a covered and handicap-accessible playground, 1.5 miles of hike/bike trails, and a fantastic spray ground. The spray ground is seasonably available for 2 to 12 year olds and is open from 9am to 9pm (closed every Wednesday for maintenance).

North / Allen
701 Angel Pkwy,
Allen 75002

214.509.4700

cityofallen.org

CELESTIAL PARK

Celestial Park is a quiet four acre park located on the Northside of Celestial Road at Bellbrook Drive. It features a jogging trail with quotes, poetry, and plant identifiers along the path. The main attraction is a large human sundial which creates a great educational opportunity.

North / Addison
5501 Celestial Rd.,
Dallas 75001

972.450.2851

addisontx.gov

CONNEMARA MEADOW PRESERVE

North / Allen
Alma Drive, South of
Bethany Drive
300 Tatum Road,
Allen 75013

214.351.0990

**connemara
conservancy.org**

Admission
Members only, except
on special open to the
public events

The Connemara Meadow Preserve is a beautiful, rich floral land that was set aside by Frances William and her daughter, Amy Monier. Concerned that their family's farmland would be overtaken by urban sprawl, they donated 72 acres as one of the first land trusts in Texas. The land is now owned and maintained by the Connemara Conservancy Foundation, a land conservation and environmental education organization.

Members on the conservancy can enjoy an area that is reminiscent of the Blackland Prairie. Non-members are invited to join on special open to the public events.

Although this book is written with the full family in mind, I am going to indulge with an adult suggestion. "Into the Meadow" is held annually in September and provides an elegant outdoor dining experience with local food.

In a bog, the water is acidic and low in nutrients. Carnivorous plants adapted to this harsh environment by gaining some of their nutrients, mainly nitrogen, from the insects and arachnids they trap and consume. Below are some of the different means in which the plants attract and trap their "prey".

- *Pitfall traps: As seen on pitcher plants, the slippery leaves make it difficult for an insect to leave and the base is filled with digestive enzymes.*

- *Flypaper: Sundews and butterworts both have sticky leaves which create an adhesive trap.*

- *Suction and Snap traps: The best known carnivorous plants, the Venus flytrap and bladderworts, have hinged leaves that snap shut when trigger hairs are touched.*

DALLAS ARBORETUM AND BOTANICAL GARDENS

The mission to open the Dallas Arboretum started in 1974 and after significant fundraising, the 66 acres of land, the DeGolyer estate, and Alex Camp homes were purchased on White Rock Lake. The "doors" opened to the public for the first time in 1984. The Arboretum and Botanical Gardens have been growing ever since. There are now over 18 different gardens, education pavilions, and plazas.

Opened in 2014, the Rory Meyers Children's Adventure Garden has quickly become a family favorite in Dallas. The garden includes more than 150 interactive exhibits, games, multiple misters (much appreciated in the Dallas heat), a tree canopy skywalk, plant petting zoo, splash pads, theater, mushroom patch, caterpillar maze, and much, much more. Check the website as there are also daily activities planned for a wide range of ages.

During the school year, many field trips make their way to the Rory Meyers Children's Adventure Garden. With this in mind, you may want to avoid weekdays before 2pm. It is also highly recommended you purchase tickets online in advance to ensure your entry (morning tickets are from 9am – 1pm and afternoon from 1pm - 5pm).

East /White Rock Lake
8525 Garland Rd,
Dallas 75218

214.515.6500

dallasarboretum.org

Admission
Adults: $15
Senior: $12
Children 3-12: $10
Children 2 and under: FREE
Children's Garden admission is $3
On-site parking: $15
(Purchase online for $8 daytime parking)

Hours
Daily: 9am to 5pm

Holidays
Closed: Thanksgiving; Christmas; and New Year's Day

Summer camp options are available for a wide range of ages. As the camp information is updated each year, check the website for the most current options and plan to register well in advance – these book up quick. Scout groups are welcome with a discounted entrance fee. Call to reserve with a two week notice at 214.515.6540.

Additional Mommy and Me, Tiny Tot, and family programs are available. For a neat adventure with older kids, check out the concert series and enjoy live music on the lawn. Be sure to stop in for the seasonal programs like Summer at the Arboretum, Autumn at the Arboretum, and the Dallas Blooms in the Spring.

DRAGON PARK

Uptown
3520 Cedar Springs
Rd., Dallas 75219

Dragon Park is very small, but worth the visit as it lets your little ones imagination go wild. Dragon Park offers unique and eclectic statues including Buddha heads, angels, fairies, gargoyles, and of course – dragons.

There are a lot of steps, so leave the strollers behind.

DUCK CREEK GREENBELT

Northeast / Garland

**dallascounty.org/
department/plandev/
trails/maps/duckgar-
land.php**

This is one of the oldest trails in the Dallas areas. It runs 5.7 miles through residential neighborhoods in Garland along the Duck Creek Greenbelt. The trail offers creek side views and connects with playgrounds.

ELM FORK NATURE PRESERVE

The Elm Fork Nature Preserve is 38 acres of undeveloped land along the Elm Fork of the Trinity River. The park includes a 14 acre pond, 9 acres of river bottom timber, 3.5 acres of wetland, and 11.5 acres of native vegetation. Canoe and kayak launch site is available. A one mile long trail starts and ends at the Interpretive Center.

North / Carrollton
Within McInnish Park,
2335 Sandy Lake Road,
Carrollton 75006

972.466.3080

cityofcarrollton.com

FAIR PARK

East / Fair Park
I-30 East: Exit 47
2nd Ave. & Fair Park

I-30 West: Exit 47C
1st Ave. & Fair Park

From Downtown:
East on Commerce,
Right on 2nd Ave.

Friends of Fair Park:
214.426.3400

fairpark.org

Parking: Free, except
for special events
DART: Fair Park
Station (Main Gate) &
MLK Station (Gate 6)

Located in the heart of Dallas, the 277 acre park is home to a variety of cultural attractions. The African-American Museum, Perot Museum of Nature and Science at Fair Park, Children's Aquarium, Hall of State, Texas Discovery Gardens, and the South Dallas Cultural Center are all located here. There are also four performance venues, including the very popular Music Hall.

In addition to the attractions at the park, you can take a swan boat across Leonhardt Lagoon for $10, enjoy a game at the Cottonbowl, or take a walking tour as there is much to see. Fair Park has the world's largest collection of 1930s Art Deco exposition buildings. Download the walking tour maps online before heading out.

While your online, sign up for the monthly e-newsletter to make sure you don't miss a beat. Also visit the Friends of Fair Park group to see how you can get involved in supporting the park.

Fair Park is a great place to visit anytime, but is most popular in the fall. Since 1886, Fair Park has hosted the annual Texas State Fair. Usually running for about three weeks, the state fair includes over 70 amusement rides, almost 400,000 square feet of exhibits, livestock and creative arts competitions, and over 200 locations serving up deep fried fair food. Visit **bigtex.com** to learn more about the fair, the daily schedule, and discounts.

FARMERS BRANCH (A CITY IN A PARK)

The town of Farmers Branch, located just northeast of Dallas off I-635, earns its nickname "A City in a Park". The small town offers 28 award-winning parks, most of which line Rawhide Creek.

Some Farmers Branch parks you should definitely put on your list: Oran Good Park (thank you for the shade sails); the Rose Gardens (mark your calendar for a spring or fall visit when over 1,500 rose bushes are in bloom); Mallon Park (excellent spot for a shady picnic); and Rawhide Park (located next to the Manske Library and provides a nice jogging path with exercise stations and an excellent old West playground).

Due to the large scale year round special events, Farmers Branch Historical Park is probably best known. The 27 acres park includes an outdoor museum, 12 historical structures, bird sanctuary, and more. While visiting Historical Park cross over Farmers Branch Lane to connect to Liberty Plaza, Denton Road Mini Park, and Gussie Field Watterworth Park behind city hall. Hint, hint - If you do plan to go to one of those big events at Historical Park take DART to the Farmers Branch Station or park at City Hall and take the trails through the connecting parks to the event.

Northeast / Farmers Branch

972.247.3131

farmersbranch.info

visitfarmersbranch. com

141

GRAPEVINE SPRINGS PRESERVE

North / Coppell
345 W. Bethel Road,
Coppell 75019

972.462.5100

dallascounty.org

Grapevine Springs is named for the springs that trickles along the rock lined channel flowing through this 16 acre preserve. In 1843, Sam Houston camped here while negotiating a peace treaty with the local Native Americans. It was officially established as a park in 1936.

JOE POOL LAKE

**South / Grand Prairie,
Cedar Hill, and
Mansfield**

joe-pool-lake.com

Joe Pool Lake is one of the most popular lakes in the DFW area and great for fishing. The 7,400 acre lake has three major parks: Cedar Hill State Park; Loyd Park; and Lynn Creek Park.

Cedar and Lynn offer camping and nice beaches. Lynn does not offer camping, but be sure to stop at the Oasis Restaurant for some peaceful dining on the water. All three parks offer hiking and biking trails, playgrounds, and other outdoor activities.

JOPPA PRESERVE

Bring your binoculars to the Joppa Preserve and watch migratory birds visit the 142 acre lake. The additional 130 acres of the woodland and prairie preserve connects to the Trinity Trail which leads to the Trinity River Audubon Center.

North / Coppell
Entrance is South of Loop 12, about ¾ mile east of SH310 before the Trinity River

214.671.0234

dallascounty.org

KATY TRAIL

Katy Trail opened in 2000 along the former Missouri, Kansas, and Texas Union Pacific railroad line. The urban trail is set above street traffic and highly prized by local residents. Enjoy the opportunity to take in amazing views of Dallas as you make your way along the wide path.

The 3.5 mile trail begins at the American Airline Center and ends south of Mockingbird Lane and Central Expressway. Planning is underway to add an additional three miles to the east connecting it to Mockingbird and White Rock DART stations.

Uptown & Highland Park

dallascounty.org

Friends of Katy Trail
katytraildallas.org

KIDD SPRINGS PARK

Oak Cliff
700 W. Canty Street,
Dallas 75201

dallasparks.org

The Kidd Springs Park offers a pool, playgrounds, garden areas, public art, and an excellent recreational center. Bring snacks for the geese and enjoy a lovely day at the park.

KIEST PARK

Oak Cliff
3080 S. Hampton Rd.
Dallas 75201
Access is off Kiest
Boulevard off
Highway 67

dallasparks.org

Established in 1930, Kiest Park is a 263.1 acre metropolitan park in South Dallas. The park includes a nice 2.8 mile paved trail that meanders through the park clinging to the edges with stops at playgrounds, athletic fields, formal gardens, picnic areas, and a recreation center.

Klyde Warren Park helps create a walkable city by connecting the Downtown Arts District with Uptown Dallas. The 5.2 acre deck park was built over the recessed Woodall Rodgers Freeway between Pearl and St. Paul streets. The park is privately managed and operated by the Woodall Rodgers Park Foundation.

Partnering with many organizations in the Art district, there is always a great variety of free classes and festivals. Located in the far Northeast corner, the Children's Park includes interactive fountains and playgrounds. Best of all is the storytelling tree and kid-size amphitheater. Mark your calendar and visit on a Tuesday when Imagination Playground blocks are available for building a mini-Dallas in the heart of Dallas.

Just west of the Children's Park is the Dallas Morning News Reading and Game Room which includes a lending library and games including checkers, backgammon, and chess.

Take a tour of the entire park by walking Jane's Lane, a 25-foot wide granite pathway lined with Red Oaks and wooden benches. There's much to discover.

Uptown/D...
2012 Woodall Rogers
Freeway, Dallas 75201

214.716.4500

klydewarrenpark.org

LAKE CLIFF PARK

Oak Cliff
300 East Colorado Boulevard, Dallas 75201

dallasparks.org

Lake Cliff Park opened on July 4, 1906 and featured an amusement park, waterslides, and a skating rink. Over the next 100+ years, the park has gone through many transitions, but is still a beloved 45 acre neighborhood park in Oak Cliff. It features playgrounds, baseball fields, garden areas, picnic tables, and Lake Cliff, a small freshwater lake.

LAKESIDE PARK

Highland Park
4601 Lakeside Drive, Dallas 75219

214.521.4161

tx-highlandpark. civicplus.com

You will feel like you have been transported to another world when strolling through Lakeside Park. The beautiful 14 acre park is exceptionally landscaped and picturesque with swans leisurely bathing in Turtle Creek.

Pack a picnic and enjoy the beauty and peace. Many bring their art supplies and set up along the creek slops to practice their still life skills.

Stop for a moment on the bridge atop Turtle Creek Dam to take it all in. Then move across to see the whimsy of the granite teddy bear sculptures.

LIBERTY PARK

Ranked one of the best playground parks in the Dallas area, Liberty Park in Plano, has a lot to offer for all ages. And thankfully, one of those offerings is shade pavilions.

North / Plano
1200 Mill Valley Road, Plano 75075

972.941.7250

parks.plano.gov

LEWISVILLE LAKE ENVIRONMENTAL LEARNING AREA (LLELA)

Lewisville Lake Environmental Learning Area offers 2,000 acres of tallgrass prairies and riparian forests in Lewisville (north central Texas about 30 minutes' drive from downtown Dallas). Elm Fork and the Trinity River pass through this native ecosystem providing fishing, canoeing, and kayaking opportunities (BYOC/K – no equipment available on site).

There are also four trails ranging from .3 to 2 miles in length that pass through hardwood forest, along the lakes and marshes, and to the 1870s Minor-Porter Log House (tours available on the 3rd Saturday per month). Primitive camping is available on Friday and Saturday nights ($10 campsites plus entry fee).

No pets allowed.

North / Lewisville
Junction of Jones Street and N. Kealy Avenue, Lewisville 75057

972.219.3930

llela.unt.edu

Admission
Adults & Seniors: $5
Children 5 and under: FREE

Hours
Friday, Saturday, & Sunday
7am to 5pm
Stays open to 7pm
March 2 - October 31

147

N STREET GARDEN PARK

Downtown
1902 Main Street,
Dallas 75201

214.744.1270

mainstreetgarden.org

This 1.75 acre park is bound by Main Street, Commerce Street, Harwood, and St. Paul. The park is Wi-Fi equipped, has a lawn space, shade structure, toddler play area, dog run, and public art instillations.

MOORE PARK

Downtown
100 Ventura Drive,
Dallas 75203

dallasparks.org

Moore Park, part of the Great Trinity Forest, was established in 1938. The 24.6 acre park includes sports fields, playground, trails, and picnic areas.

In 2013, a new bridge across Cedar Creek connected Moore Park to the Santa Fe Trestle Trail. A new plaza entryway features a 25 foot overlook and an elevated walkway to the terraced grove of oak trees.

OAK POINT PARK & NATURE PRESERVE

Be mindful of wild animals as you explore Plano's largest park. The 800-acre Oak Point Park and Nature Preserve includes 3.5 miles of concrete trails and five miles of soft surface trails located along Rowlett Creek. The trails are well marked and good for all skill levels. Bring your binoculars for a great birding experience in the wooded and backland prairie areas.

North / Plano
5901 Los Rios Blvd.,
Plano 75074

plano.gov

PLANO TRAILS

There are 70 recreational trail miles in Plano. A detailed Park and Trail map is available on the website which provides total miles per trail and round trip/one-way descriptions. You and your family may particularly enjoy the Arbor Hills Nature Preserve, Russell Creek Park, and the Bob Woodruff / Santa Fe trails.

North / Plano

plano.gov

PLEASANT OAKS PARK

Southeast
8701 Greenmound
Ave., Dallas 75227

214.670.0941

dallasparks.org

Enjoy a full day of activities at the Pleasant Oaks Park. The 18.7 acre community park and recreation center offers swimming, tennis, and playgrounds for all ages. Flanked by big trees and a huge climbing net, this park is a winner for kids who have the drive to climb.

QUORUM PARK

North / Addison
1601 Westgrove Drive,
Addison 75001

West side of Quorum
Drive between West-
grove Drive and Keller
Springs

addisontx.gov

Quorum Park is one of Addison's favorite parks – especially at night when you can take a relaxing family stroll while enjoying the lit fountains.

REVERCHON PARK

Originally named Turtle Creek Park it was renamed after Julien Reverchon, a well-known Dallas botanist and member or LaReunion. The park celebrated its 100 year anniversary in 2015 and over the years it has grown to 46 acres. It includes multiple baseball fields, playgrounds, and gardens. Seasonal events, such as the Great Texas Food Truck Rally and One Run, are held here. The park connects to Katy Trail.

N. of Victory Park / W. of Uptown
Maple Avenue and Turtle Creek Blvd, Dallas 75202

214.670.7721

reverchonpark friends.com

Julien Reverchon

A herbarium, sometimes known as a herbar, is a collection of preserved plant species. It may include the whole plant or just plant parts that are usually dried and mounted on a sheet.

Herbaria assist in the study of plant taxonomy and can be used to catalogue the flora in an area, including the historical changes in the vegetation over time.

Julien Reverchon had collected more than 2,600 species and 20,000 specimens of Texas plants prior to his death in 1905. Today his herbarium is kept at the Missouri Botanical Garden in St. Louis.

ROBERT E. LEE PARK

Uptown
3333 Turtle Creek
Boulevard
Dallas 75219

214.526.7664

dallasparks.org

Established in 1909, the Robert E. Lee Park is an immaculate 14.1 acre park located in Uptown with connection to Turtle Creek Trail. It features a replica of the Curtis-Lee Mansion in Arlington, VA. The park does not have a playground, but is very dog friendly and provides nice walkways for strollers.

ROWLETT CREEK NATURE PRESERVE TRAILS

**Far Northeast /
Rowlett, TX**
Miller Rd. &
Dexham Rd.,
Rowlett 75088

972.412.6145

ci.rowlett.tx.us

You will find a 14.2 mile loop of hiking trails with native areas, pond, and picnic tables at the Rowlett Creek Nature Preserve Trails. The Rowlett trails are very popular for mountain biking and trail running, but not really the best for those pushing a stroller.

TRINITY FOREST AND RIVER

The 7,000 acres of the Great Trinity Forest is the largest urban bottomland hardwood forest in the United States (about six times the size of Central Park in New York).

Southeast

trinityriver corridor.com

Dallas has been working hard to create and use a long term management plan to address tree conservation, protection of wild life, and to create public access for hiking and camping.

See more information in the Moore Park and Trinity River Audubon Center sections.

TRINITY RIVER AUDUBON CENTER

Southeast
6500 Great Trinity
Forest Way
(formerly S. Loop 12)
Dallas 75217

214-398-8722

**trinityriver.
audubon.org**

Admission
Adults: $6
Senior: $4
Children 3-12: $3
Children 2 and under:
FREE

Free for TRAC
Members

FREE the third
Thursday / month

Group rates available

Hours
Monday: Closed
Tuesday – Saturday:
9am to 4pm
Sunday: 10am to 5pm

Holidays
Closed on major
holidays.
Check website or call
ahead to verify holiday
hours and special late
night events.

The 7000 acre Great Trinity Forest is the largest urban hardwood forest in the United States. It supports a variety of plant and animal species. Just eight minutes southeast of downtown Dallas, The Trinity River Audubon Center welcomes you into this amazing forest.

Enjoy five miles of nature viewing trails, almost all of which are wheelchair accessible. A trail map is available on the website and in the Center. The trails explore three eco-systems: wetlands; forest; and prairie. Bring your binoculars as there are over 60 resident bird species and 200 migrants who pass through on the journey between Canada and Mexico.

Besides birds, you will be able to visit other pollinators. There are six colonies of bee hives and you can take a taste of their delicious honey. A butterfly garden is also open to the public.

Stop by the eco-friendly Center for a conservation class, to visit the indoor exhibit hall with native animals, or to pick up animal scat ID cards before you head out on the trails. You can even take in a movie at the amphitheater and purchase unique and locally made gifts at the Nature Store.

Nature Club, available for kids 5-12, runs fall through spring with one session per month. The club costs $200 for members, slightly more for non-members, and has a monthly nature focus and activity the third Sunday per month for two hours.

Discover workshops are available throughout the year with a $15 fee per participant. The two hour long workshops require a minimum of 10 people and encourage team work in the outdoors.

Birding classes, teacher workshops, and field trip options are available. Birthday Parties are also available and include one hour of educator-led outdoor bird, bug, or butterfly investigation.

Habitat Restoration Day is a really interesting and educational volunteer opportunity for children 11 years and older. It is held the second Saturday of every month from 9am to 12pm. Additional family volunteer opportunities include becoming a Butterfly Gardener or joining a Special Events Team.

Special events are planned throughout the year. Be sure to mark your calendar for Owl-O-Ween! See the website for additional information for special events and volunteer opportunities.

Most trails are wheelchair accessible and the center is accessible by wheelchair. The front desk can assist with special needs questions (214.309.5801).

TRINITY RIVER EXPEDITIONS

Southeast
304 Lyman Circle,
Dallas 75211

214.941.1757

canoedallas.com

Rates
Start at $40;
Guided canoe trips
available for $45

Schedule varies
by season.
Check website or call.

There are over 100 miles of canoe trips available in the Upper Trinity Basin. The Trinity River Expeditions team can make your adventure a reality. They offer canoe and boat rentals (multi-day available), shuttles if you have your own boats, and guided tours.

TURTLE CREEK GREENBELT

**Highland Park
to Oak Lawn**
4700 Drexel Drive,
Dallas 75202

Turtle Creek is an excellent place to enjoy the colors of fall. Turtle Creek Greenbelt connects three parks as the 2 mile trail meanders through Highland Park to Oak Lawn. The greenbelt also connects to Katy Trail at the Robert E. Lee and Reverchon parks.

WHITE ROCK CREEK TRAIL

White Rock Creek Trail is a north-south trail that connects North Dallas to the tip of White Rock Lake. If you park at Valley View Park off Hillcrest Road (north of I-635), you can take the lake loop and circle back for a 25-mile trip. Additional entry points to consider are Greenville and Royal and off Merriman Road near Abrams.

North to East

WHITE ROCK LAKE

White Rock Lake was built in the early 1900s to serve as a much needed water source for the growing town of Dallas. Soon after the first water was pumped from the reservoir in 1913, the people of Dallas realized the White Rock Lake area was also perfect for outdoor recreation.

East
8100 Doran Circle,
Dallas 75238

214.670.8740

whiterocklake.org

On December 13, 1929, White Rock Lake and the surrounding land officially became a city park. The first permanent lakeside amenity to open was the Bath House and Bathing Beach on the eastern shore. Today, the Bath House serves as a cultural center (see more information in the Arts & Museums chapter of this guide).

Parking is available off Buckner Boulevard, Mockingbird Lane, and West Lawther Drive.

White Rock Lake is probably the best known and most visited park in Dallas. The 1,015 acre city park includes over nine miles of hike/bike trails, rental facilities, boat ramps, a dog park, bird watching areas, and excellent playgrounds.

Are We There Yet? Dallas

Take Me Out to the Ballgame

Have you heard of the Dallas Cowboys? Texas Rangers? Dallas Mavericks? If not, you have been living under a rock for quite some time. Learn more about the great pro sport options in Dallas, Arlington, and Frisco in this chapter.

But don't just watch the pros, there are lot of options for kids to get in the game. Be sure to check on options at your local parks and recreation department, YMCA, or the various sports academies in Dallas.

Dallas Parks and Recreation Department
214.671.1490
dallasparks.org

DALLAS COWBOYS (NFL)

Far West / Arlington
One Legends Way,
Arlington 76011

dallascowboys.com

Admission for games:
Tickets through
Ticketmaster

**Tours of the AT&T
Stadium are offered
daily:**
$17 and up / Group
pricing for 20 or more.

Cheer for "America's Team" at a game or just plan a visit to the amazing AT&T stadium. The Stadium Art Tour focuses on the museum quality contemporary art with 46 works by established and emerging artists. Fourteen of the pieces were commissioned specifically for the stadium.

Self-guided tours provide access to the locker rooms and the field where you can pass through at your leisure. VIP Guided Tours include access to the post-game interview room and private suites.

If going to see a game, plan to get there early and enjoy the Kids Zone which opens two hours prior to kick off and is free of charge with game ticket purchase. The Kids Zone provides interactive games, giveaways, face painting, and zip lines.

The Cowboys also offer Youth Camps throughout Dallas. CAMP Cowboys and CAMP Dallas Cowboys Cheerleaders for children age 7 and up. The cost for the one to five day camps range $150 to $350.

Cowboys Trivia

Match to the Cowboy to the accomplishment

a. Roger Staubach
b. Troy Aikman
c. Bob Lilly

d. Tony Dorsett
e. Michael Irvin
f. Emmitt Smith

1. Cowboys all-time leading passer.

2. Led the Cowboys to a win over the Denver Broncos in Super Bowl XII.

3. In 1995, set an NFL record for most 100-yard receiving games in a season.

4. A year after retirement, he was the first inductee into the Cowboy's "Ring of Honor".

5. As a Cowboy, he rushed for more than 1,000 yards in 11 straight seasons becoming the NFL's all-time leading rusher in 2002.

6. Nicknamed "Captain Comeback" for his ability to overcome fourth-quarter deficits.

6. a
5. f
4. c
3. e
2. d
1. b

DALLAS DESPERADOS

Far West / Irving
Cowboys Center, One
Cowboys Parkway,
Irving 75063

972.556.9333

dallasdesperados.com

The Dallas Desperados are an Arena Football League extension team of the Dallas Cowboys. Game times and prices are available online.

DALLAS MAVERICKS BASKETBALL CLUB (NBA)

An NBA game is truly an amazing experience for both young and old. To stay within a tight budget, check on the website for special ticket offers. Family Nights, Military, and 1st Responders options are available. You may even be able to sing your way to a game. Upload a video of your talented singer through Facebook to audition to sing the National Anthem at a game.

Besides the games, the Mavericks offer unique opportunities for young basketball players. Hoop Camp is available throughout the Dallas area (M-F from 9am to 4pm for $240). Every year the Mavs pick 80 Ballkids (ages 12 to 17) from the Mavericks Hoop Camp to participate in various game night responsibilities.

If you've got a real fan on your hands, consider joining the Mavs Kids Club Free at nba.com/mavericks/mavs-kids-club to receive quarterly newsletters, monthly giveaways, special contests, events, invitations, and discounts.

Victory Park
American Airlines
Center
2500 Victory Ave,
Dallas 75219

214.222.9687

nba.com/mavericks

Check game schedule and buy tickets online.

DART: Take the Green line to Victory Station.

163

DALLAS POLO CLUB

Far South / Red Oak
730 Bent Trail,
Red Oak 75154

214.979.0300

dallaspoloclub.org

The Dallas Polo Club is located at the Bear Creek Polo Ranch, about thirty minutes south of Dallas. Check online for the schedule of polo matches open to the public. There is usually at least one planned per month. The outdoor season is April through mid-November. Indoor arena matches are held through winter and early spring.

The website provides information on lessons as well!

DALLAS STARS HOCKEY CLUB (NHL)

While you are checking out the game dates for the Dallas Stars Hockey team, be sure to take a look at the Dallas Stars Foundation. Learn more about the various community programs including grants, scholarships, education, and fitness programs online through the Community link. One of my favorite programs is Little Rookies, a free hockey trial camp for first-time hockey players at the Star Center rinks in and around Dallas.

If you've got a hockey fan on your hands, be sure to join the Dallas Stars Kids Club. The $10 membership includes two game tickets, a jersey lunch bag, free public skating at Dr Pepper Star Centers, discounts, and other promotional items.

The Star Centers also host hockey camps, figure skating clinics, birthday parties, group broomball, and ice shows.

Star Center Rinks:

- Euless: 1400 South Pipleline, Eules, 76040 (817) 267-4233

- Farmers Branch: 12700 N Stemmons Fwy, Farmers Branch, 75234 (214) 432-3131

- Frisco: 2601 Avenue of the Stars, Frisco, 75034 (214) 387-5600

- McKinney:6993 Stars Ave, McKinney, 75070 (469) 675-8325

- Plano: 4020 West Plano Parkway, Plano, 75093 (972) 758-7528

- Valley Ranch: 211 Cowboys Parkway, Irving, 75063 (972) 444-0540

- Richardson: 522 Centennial Blvd., Richardson, 75081 (972) 680-7525

Victory Park
American Airlines Center
2500 Victory Ave
Dallas 75219

214.467.8277

stars.nhl.com

Admission & Game Schedule are available online.
Ticket prices range from range from $25 to $150

Be sure to check the Fan Zone for ticket specials, contests, and promotional give-aways.

DART to the American Airlines Center: Take the Green line to Victory Station.

165

DEVIL'S BOWL SPEEDWAY

East / Mesquite
1711 Lawson Road,
Mesquite 75181

972.222.2421

devilsbowl.com

Admission
Adults: $12
Children 12 and under:
FREE!

Every Saturday night from mid-March through October, your family can enjoy exciting dirt track races at the Devil's Bowl Speedway. The pit gate opens at 5pm, grandstands at 6pm, and the racing starts at 8:30pm. Choose from over 10,000 seats to have an unobstructed view of the D shaped track.

FC DALLAS SOCCER CLUB (MLS)

The Toyota Stadium and Toyota Soccer Center is a 145-acre multipurpose sports and entertainment facility. It is one of the top venues for pro and amateur soccer.

Be sure to participate in your local library's reading program to receive complimentary tickets to FC Dallas games as a prize. Additional tickets for friends and family are available at a discounted rate.

FC Dallas has the highest rated US Soccer Development Academy in the nation. The School of Excellence Soccer Camps are attended by players from all over the world. There are various levels available for ages 6-16. Act quick as the weekly camps sell out fast. Starting at $150 and up per week. Register online: fcdallas.com/youth/camps

North / Frisco
Toyota Stadium,
9200 World Cup Way,
Frisco 75034

469.365.0000

fcdallas.com

Single game admission starts at $20.

Check out the FCD Express: Two tickets and two round-trip bus tickets to the stadium starting at $32.

FRISCO ROUGH RIDERS (MILB)

North / Frisco
Dr. Pepper Ballpark,
7300 Rough Riders
Trail, Frisco 75034

972.731.9200

milb.com

Check out the RoughRiders, official Minor League Baseball team, play at the very family friendly Dr Pepper Ballpark in Frisco. Behind the scenes tours of the Ballpark are available Monday – Friday between 10am and 3pm during the season ($9 per person and includes tickets for an upcoming game).

Check the schedule online for special discounted games.

Children ages 9-12 can sign up for the RoughRiders Baseball Academy.

A free ticket will be sent the month of your child's birthday if they join Deuce's Birthday Club (children under 12).

GRAND PRAIRIE AIRHOGS

West / Grand Prairie
1600 Lone Star
Parkway,
Grand Prairie 75050

972.595.7380

airhogsbaseball.com

Enjoy an American Association Baseball Game with the AirHogs. The stadium is located about 20 minutes West of Downtown Dallas in Grand Prairie. Baseball clinics are available for the little ones.

LONE STAR PARK

The Lone Star Park opened in May 1996. In its first year, almost 400,000 patrons visited the park and this was even before the first live horse race. The true action started in April 1997, when Henry White and Hugh Fitzsimmons' I Are Sharp, at odds of 49-1, won the first race with more than twenty thousand fans in attendance. Over the years, the enthusiasm for the track and the sport has continued to grow.

Located about 20 minutes west of Downtown Dallas in Grand Prairie, The Lone Star Park, will be sure to provide an exciting outing for you and your family. Check the online calendar for race details. On select nights, enjoy a free concert with the price of general admission.

West / Grand Prairie
1000 Lone Star
Parkway,
Grand Prairie 75050

972.263.RACE

General Admission: $5

MESQUITE CHAMPIONSHIP RODEO

For twelve weeks, hold onto your hats when the Professional Rodeo Cowboys come to Mesquite, Texas. Thousands of visitors will flock to the Mesquite Arena between June through August to watch the bareback riding, steer wrestling, roping, and racing.

Tickets available through Ticketmaster or by calling the arena. Admission varies by seat and event.

East / Mesquite
Mesquite Arena
1818 Rodeo Drive,
Mesquite 75149

972.285.8777

mesquiterodeo.com

TEXAS RANGERS

West / Arlington
Globe Life Park,
1000 Ballpark Way,
Arlington 76011

817-273-5222

texas.rangers.mlb.com

The Texas Rangers played their first game in Texas on April 15, 1972. As part of the American League Western Division of Major League Baseball, the Rangers won the 1996, 1998, and 1999 AL Western Division championships. The team struggled for much of the early 2000s. In 2010, the Rangers advanced to the their first postseason since 1999 and faced the San Francisco Giants in the 2010 World Series. The Rangers lost the Series 4-1, but were back on track. In 2011, they again made it to the World Series, but proceeded to lose to the St. Louis Cardinals.

Support and attendance at the Globe Life Park in Arlington continues to grow. The park is about a 20 minute trip from downtown Dallas (traffic can double this time, so plan accordingly). Get ready for the trip by downloading free coloring pages of Captain, the Rangers Mascot.

If you have the luxury of picking any game, be sure to check the schedule for special events, such as: post-game fireworks shows or concerts; ice cream nights; autograph nights; military appreciation days; family days; fan appreciation days; and give away nights.

Ballpark tours are available throughout the year and start at the First Base Box Office. These include a behind-the-scenes look at the batting cages, press box, dugout, and more. Tour tickets do not need to be purchased in advance, but it is wise to do so just in case. The price is $14 for adults, $11 for students and seniors, $7 for children 4-14, and free for 4 and under. For tour information, you can contact 817.273.5099.

Jr. Rangers club membership is available for $20 (ages 13 and under). Kids receive a bag, baseball, VIP membership, four ticket vouchers, and 15% discount at the gift shop.

The Youth Ballpark is located directly north of Rangers Ballpark in Arlington (1201 Nolan Ryan Expressway, Arlington 76011). Plan an awesome birthday party for $125/hour (two hour minimum). The price includes a $50 food and beverage credit at the concession stands.

Camps at the Youth Ballpark

Rookie Camps:

- Available for children 5 to 6 years old
- 4 days, 3 hours per day for $180 and up

All-Skills Camps:

- 7-12 years / players who have not had much experience, but are eager to learn.
- 4 days, 3.5 hours per day for $200

Development Camps and pitching clinics are also available. One Day Clinics for various purposes, ages, and experiences: $50 and up. Book your child in a camp quickly as they tend to sell out fast.

Are We There Yet? Dallas

Trains, Planes, and Automobiles

Kids love trains, planes, and automobiles. Fuel their intrinsic love of all things mobile by visiting these great locations in and around the Big D.

ACADEMY OF MODEL AERONAUTICS

modelaircraft.org

The Academy of Model Aeronautics (AMA) website provides helpful information about clubs in the Dallas area.

Children under 19 can join AMA for free. Clubs often offer classes for beginners. Those interested in aviation or model planes will surely enjoy the club benefits (scholarship awards, free admission to the National Model Aviation Museum in IN, Expo admissions and more).

The online events calendar provides a list of dates and locations for demonstrations, competitions, and more. Even just watching a club meet and fly is an exciting experience.

DALLAS AREA KITEFLIERS ORGANIZATION (DAKO)

dako.us

The Dallas Area Kitefliers Organization (DAKO) is a family club welcome to anyone who wishes to join. Even if your child is not interested in joining the club, the website provides upcoming fly dates. Watching the members fly single line, two line, three line, and quad line kites at various parks in and around Dallas can make for an enjoyable afternoon.

Dako is the Japanese name for kite.

DALLAS FIREFIGHTER'S MUSEUM

The fire house at Fair Park was an active station which opened in 1907. In the late 60s, the Dallas Fire Council approved formation of a fire museum using the Fair Park station for this purpose. Opening in 1972, the museum provides fire safety education, honors fallen heroes, and preserves firefighting history. Vintage tools and memorabilia are on display, including "Old Tige", a 600-gallons-per-minute pumper that was in use in Dallas until 1921.

At time of publication, the museum is undergoing a large campaign to raise funds to add an IMAX theatre, more hands-on exhibits, and purchase additional antique equipment. For more information on the campaign and progress, contact 214.821.1500.

Fire Safety & Education:
Visit the Sparky the Fire Dog website at **sparky.org.** The site provides great fire safety and educational videos, activities, safety checklists, cartoons, and more.

East / Fair Park
(Across from the main entrance to Fair Park)
3801 Parry Avenue,
Dallas 75226

214.821.1500

dallasfiremuseum.com

Admission
Adults: $4
Children: $2

Hours
Monday, Tuesday, & Sunday: Closed
Wed. – Sat.:
9am to 4pm

In the early 1800s, fire engines were pulled by firemen. An 1832 yellow fever epidemic created the need to utilize horses to pull engines. The use caused quite a stir and often embarrassment as the engines pulled by men often beat horse pulled engines to the scene. However, due to the added size and weight of steam engines, firefighters reluctantly started to use horses. Before long, horses started to live in the stations and were accepted as part of the team.

These horses had to be carefully selected. They had to be strong, obedient, calm, and fearless. Once arriving at a fire, they had to wait patiently as flames and embers surrounded them. Some cities trained the horses on the job, while others had "horse colleges" equip with training stalls, feed rooms, and a horse hospital. The fire station at Fair Park was the first horse hospital for the Dallas Fire Department.

DALLAS ZOO / MONORAIL SAFARI

South of Downtown
650 South R.L. Thorn-
ton Freeway (I-35E
take Marsalis exit),
Dallas 75203

469.554.7500

dallaszoo.com

Zoo Admission:
Adults: $15
Senior: $12 ($5 admis-
sion on Wednesdays)
Children 3 - 11: $12
Children 2 and under:
FREE

Your train lover, will be delighted with
a ride on the Monorail Safari which
provides a one-mile tour through six
habitats. See more information about the
Dallas Zoo in the Animals All Around
chapter.

FOUNDERS' PLAZA
PLANE OBSERVATION AREA

NW / DFW Airport
1700 N Airfield Drive,
Irving, TX 75261 (Exit
on Highway 114 and
head south on Texan
Trail to N. Airfield
Drive)

972.973.5270

**dfwairport.com/
founders**

Hours
Daily: 7am to 7pm

Founders' Plaza is small and simple, yet
a favorite spot for aviation enthusiasts.
Located on the North size of the
Dallas Fort Worth (DFW) Airport, the
Observation Area provides wonderful
views of the aircrafts coming and going.

There are telescopes, broadcasts of the
control tower operators, commemorative
monuments, and statues. Although
the aircrafts are noisy, the place is
surprisingly peaceful with picnic benches
and a nice grassy area.

FRISCO FIRE SAFETY TOWN

Take a walk around a miniature version of the town of Frisco while learning about crosswalk safety, seatbelt safety, and wearing helmets. Safety Town also includes a safety house with realistic living space where children can learn more about home hazards.

Classroom opportunities provide information on weather safety and emergency situations. Classes are booked online. Unless a special event is planned, call to reserve a time for the Safety Town tour.

Visit the website often for special event opportunities and times. Some family favorites include Trick-Or-Treat and Holiday Lights.

North / Frisco
8601 Gary Burns Drive, Frisco 75034

972.292.6350
(Call ahead tour appointments required)

ci.frisco.tx.us/ safetytown

Admission: FREE!

Hours
Monday - Friday: 8am to 5pm

FRONTIERS OF FLIGHT MUSEUM

NW / Near Dallas Love Field
6911 Lemmon Avenue, Dallas 75209

214.350.3600

flightmuseum.com

Admission
Adults: $10
Senior: $8
Children 3 - 17: $7
Children 3 and under:
FREE

Hours
Monday - Saturday:
10am to 5pm
Sunday: 1pm to 5pm

Holidays
Closed: New Year's Day, Thanksgiving, Christmas Eve, and Christmas Day

Check website or call ahead to verify hours as the museum is occasionally closed for special events.

The Frontiers of Flight Museum is a 100,000 square-foot facility that provides a great way to explore the history of aviation. The museum displays over 30 aircraft and space vehicles, including early fliers from the Wright Brothers, artifacts from the Hindenburg, and the Apollo 7 spacecraft. Enjoy an awesome photo opportunity in the Space Flight gallery with a full-size reproduction of the Soviet Union's Sputnik I flying overhead.

Kids will enjoy the main galleries and exhibits, but it will be even harder to tear them away from the children's discovery area. This area is complete with a child size plane, amphitheater, climbing tower control structure, aviation books, and hands-on-opportunities. Party rentals are available for a unique birthday experience.

The classes and summer camps are inspiring with age appropriate opportunities starting with PreK through 10th grade. Consider the amazing learning and fun that can take place in classes on aerodynamics with paper airplanes, history of space flight, how the airport works, scale models, and exploring the solar system.

H. Ross Perot Jr. and Jay Corburn of Dallas made the 1st around the world helicopter flight.
They did this in the "Spirit of Texas" in September 1982.

GRAPEVINE VINTAGE RAILROAD

The Grapevine Vintage Railroad offers a variety of seasonal and special train experiences throughout the year. The North Pole Express, Halloween Treat Train, and Saturday Morning Fun Trains are a real delight for any child who has fallen in love with trains. Feeling extra adventurous? Check out the Great Train Robberies schedule.

Prices vary by train ride (special trips, ticket class and one way vs. round trip). The price provided is for a round trip ride from Grapevine to the Ft. Worth Stockyards.

Grapevine, TX and Ft. Worth Stockyards Station

817.410.8136

grapevinetexasusa. com/grapevine-vintage-railroad

Admission
Adults: $30
Children: $10

Grapevine Station:
705 South Main Street, Grapevine, 76051

Monday - Wednesday: Closed

Friday: 10am to 5pm

Saturday: 9am to 5pm

Sunday: 11am to 5pm

Ft. Worth Stockyards Station:
130 East Exchange Ave, Ft. Worth 76164

Monday - Friday: Closed

Saturday - Sunday: 1:30pm to 4pm

MCKINNEY AVENUE TROLLEY (M-LINE)

Uptown
Streetcars run on 2.8 mile track through the charming shopping and dining Uptown Dallas district

214.855.0006

mata.org

Admission: FREE

The M-Line provides free transportation on restored vintage trolleys in the uptown neighborhood. The trolleys run 365 days a year. Check the schedule online and enjoy your ride.

Consider chartering a trolley for your kids' next birthday party! Chartered trolley ride is $200 for two hours.

MUSEUM OF THE AMERICAN RAILROAD

North / Frisco
Interim Offices:
6455 Page Street,
Frisco 75034

214.428.0101

museumofthe americanrailroad.org

Admission
Adults: $7
Senior: $7
Children 3 - 12: $3
Children 3 and under:
FREE

The museum, which opened in Fair Park in 1963, is currently relocating to Frisco. The move is taking places in phases and at the time of publication, Frisco's Heritage Museum is providing interim space for the railroad museum. The future site will include over one mile of track for the rolling stock collection, a visitor center, exhibition halls, and a special events facility. The future will also bring a roundhouse and turntable.

Walking tours are currently available on Thursdays and Saturdays at 11am and 1pm.

Check website or call ahead for new hours once the move is complete.

The Traditional Fun Zones

Looking for the best roller coaster, old fashion arcades, or the perfect waterpark? This is the chapter for you!

ADVENTURE LANDING

North
17717 Coit Rd,
Dallas 75252

972.248.4653

**adventurelanding.
com/parks/dallas/**

Hours
Monday - Thursday:
10am to 10pm
Friday:
10am to Midnight
Saturday:
9am to Midnight
Sunday: 10am to 10pm

Adventure Landing offers bumper boats, batting cages, an arcade, 18 hole miniature golf, laser tag, and go karts. Some restrictions apply for age and height.

Party packages are available starting at $13.99 per person (8 person minimum).

Prices vary by attraction. Check online for special deals, like the all you can play days and super Saturdays. The site also provides discounts for online purchases and daily specials.

AMAZING JAKE'S FOOD AND FUN

Far North / Plano
831 North Central Expressway, Plano 75075

972.509.5253

**amazingjakes
plano.com**

Hours
Sunday - Thursday:
10am to 9pm
Friday: 10am to 11pm
Saturday:
10am to 11pm

Amazing Jake's in Plano offers go-karts, laser tag, miniature golf, bumper cars, and climbing walls. Jake's also has video games and a fan favorite for those 42" tall or more is the 3D movie ride.

The all-u-can-eat buffet includes pizza, pasta, soups, salad bar, and desserts. The buffet is available one hour after open until one hour before close.

Prices vary by package type. A Family Package costs $40 and includes four buffets and four $5 Fun Cards.

Check online for special deals, information about joining the coupon club, and birthday party packages.

BAHAMA BEACH WATERPARK

Just ten minutes from downtown, the Bahama Beach waterpark can help you cool down and relax. Sit back and enjoy a ride in the lazy river or be more adventurous on the 45 foot tall slide.

Coconut Cove provides a rain fortress playground complete with pulleys, water buckets, three slides, and a 1,000 gallon dumping bucket (40 inches tall to ride slides unsupervised). Birthday parties and group rates are available. Season passes are available for $60.

$2 off per ticket for Dallas residents.

Hours are subject to change based on the time of the year and weather. Please call ahead.

Southwest
1895 Campfire Circle,
Dallas 75232

214.671.0820

**bahamabeach
dallas.com**

Admission
Adults & Seniors: $15
Under 48" tall: $11
Children 2 and under:
FREE

Hours
Tuesday – Saturday:
10am to 6pm
Sunday: Noon to 6pm

BOUNCE U

Offering open bounce times, family bounce times, and birthday parties.

WOW – take note! Parent's Night Out! Reserve a spot to drop your children off. Available every other Friday from 6pm to 10pm ($20 for the 1st child/ $18 for each additional child).

Far North / Plano
2532 Summit Avenue,
Plano 75074

972.422.3399

bounceu.com

Admission
Various package prices
available online.
Open bounce times $10

CELEBRATION STATION

Far East / Mesquite
4040 Towne Crossing
Blvd., Mesquite 75150

972.279.7888

celebrationstation.com

Hours
Monday - Thursday:
10am to 11pm
Friday – Saturday:
10am to 12am
Sunday: 11am to 10pm

Celebration Station is located in Mesquite (about 20 minutes west of downtown Dallas). The station offers arcade games, batting cages, bumper boats, go-karts, laser tag, miniature golf, and climbing walls. There is a restaurant with the normal ballpark type food selection. Check online for coupons and specials.

Admission
Cost varies by entertainment package. Check the website for daily specials, such as unlimited outdoor rides on Tuesdays and double your fun on Wednesdays. Family Fun Day is on Thursdays with unlimited outdoor rides and pizza buffet for $15.99.

COSMIC JUMP TRAMPOLINE ENTERTAINMENT CENTER

North / Allen
1300 N Central
Expressway, Suite 300
Allen 75013

Far Northwest / Lewisville
1915 S Stemmons Freeway (I-35N),
Lewisville 75067

214.383.1400

cosmicjump.com

Cosmic Jump provides birthday parties, open jump time, trampoline dodgeball leagues, and slam dunk trampoline basketball events. Their claim to fame… the longest freestyle trampolines in Dallas.

Admission and Hours:

Monday - Thursday: Noon to 8pm / $12 for 2 hours, $4 for each additional hour

Friday: Noon to 11pm / $12 for 2 hours, $4 for each additional hour

Saturday: 10am to 11pm / $12 for first hour, $6 for each additional hour

Sunday & Holidays: 10 am to 6pm / $12 for first hour, $6 for each additional hour

FORT PAINTBALL

Fort Paintball is located on 30 acres in Parker Texas (across the street from the South Fork Ranch). Seven different paintball fields are available. Reservations and group rates are available. The minimum playing age is 10 years old.

North / Allen
4404 Dillehay Drive,
Allen 75002

214.929.0256

fortpaintball.com

Admission
$25-$40 package prices

Hours
Saturday - Sunday:
10am to 6pm

Open additional days
in the summer.

HAWAIIAN FALLS ADVENTURE PARK

Wave pool, daring slides, and lazy river will delight your family on a hot summer day. Kids under 12 will have a blast at the massive interactive rain forest, Keiki Kove. Season passes, birthday party options, and private cabanas are available.

Far North /
The Colony
4400 Paige Road,
The Colony 75056

888.544.7550

www.hfalls.com

Admission
Adults: $27
Senior: $20
Children under 48"
tall: $20

Hours
Daily: 10:30am to 6pm
Open late Spring
through early Fall

185

Are We There Yet? Dallas

INDOOR SAFARI PARK

**Far Northwest /
Flower Mound**
2301 Cross Timber
Road, Suite 175,
Flower Mound
75028

972.355.7200

**indoorplayground-
fortworth.com**

Hours
Monday – Saturday:
10am to 6pm
Sunday:
Noon to 6pm

The special at the Indoor Safari Park is definitely birthday parties. There are multiple themes to choose from (robotic animal rides, safari train ride, and ceramic painting to name a few). The park also offers "Beat the Heat" indoor camps and open play times that include miniature golf and a jungle gym.

Check the website or call ahead to verify prices and availability for parties/open play time.

LIL NINJAS

**North /
Farmers Branch**
4601 McEwen Road,
Farmers Branch 75244

972.385.7467

lilninjasdallas.com

Admission:
Ages 2 – 4:
$10 for 2 hours,
$6 each additional
hour
Ages 5+:
$17 for 2 hours,
$9 each additional
hour

Indoor, climate controlled environment for children to challenge themselves on unique obstacle courses, including two regulation sized dodgeball courts and basketball hoops. Birthday party options available.

Check site for admission and hours based on seasonal offerings.

Hours:
Monday – Thursday: 10am to 6pm
Friday: 10am to 8pm
Saturday: 11am to 8pm
Sunday: 11am to 7pm

186

LUNAR MINI GOLF

The name says it all...Stop in to enjoy glow in the dark miniature golf. Birthday packages are available ($99 for 12 players with 90 minutes of unlimited golf and use of the Party Zone).

Far North / Plano
811 N Central Expy,
Plano 75075

843.461.6190

glowminigolf.com

Hours
Monday - Thursday: Closed
Friday: 3pm to 9pm
Saturday: 10am to 9pm
Sunday: Noon to 6pm
Extended hours in summer.
Check website or call ahead to verify hours and specials.

Admission
Adults: $9
Children 6 - 12: $8
Children 3 - 5: $6
Children 2 and under: FREE

Sign up on website to receive coupons.

MAIN EVENT

Mini golf, rock climbing, laser tag, karaoke, bowling, bocce ball, and video games are available at Main Event in Frisco. Birthday parties and special events offerings are available.

Far North / Frisco
9375 Dallas Parkway,
Frisco 75033

469.362.7227

mainevent.com

Hours
Monday: 9am to 2am
Tuesday – Thursday: 9am to 12am
Friday & Saturday: 9am to 2am
Sunday: 9am to 12am

Check website or call ahead to verify seasonal hours.

Admission
Check online for various package prices, happy hours, and specials.

187

POLE POSITION RACEWAY

Far North / Frisco
10550 John W. Elliot Drive, Frisco 75033

972.727.7223

poleposition-raceway.com/dallas-frisco

Admission
Adults: $22
Children 56"+: $20
Children 48" to 55" tall: $18

Must be 48" tall to race.

Pole Position Raceway in Frisco offers indoor go karts in a climate controlled environment. The drive time is approximately 10 minutes. Adult go-karts are for children over 56" tall and kid's karts are available for children at least 48" tall.

Group event and birthday packages are available.

Membership packages are available, the cost provided is for non-member racing.

Hours
Monday - Thursday: 11am to 10pm
Friday: 11am to 11pm
Saturday: 10am to 11pm
Sunday: 10am to 8pm

PUMP IT UP

Locations throughout the Dallas Area

pumpitupparty.com

Open Jump Admission and Hours:
Check location for specifics

Specializing in birthday parties, Pump It Up, offers inflatables and bounce houses. Open Jump times are also available.

SANDY LAKE AMUSEMENT PARK

Sandy Lake Amusement Park is a great place to introduce little ones to the exhilaration of an amusement ride. There are multiple rides with minimum height restrictions starting at 32". There are also a hand full of larger rides for older kids.

The character and prices at Sandy Lake bring you back to the 70s. Skee ball machines still take a quarter and a pony ride will run about 75 cents. The amusement park feels like a small state fair, just in a permanent location.

A train circles the park with a delightful conductor spinning yarns about the history of the trees and animals on the property. Take a walk around to see the peacocks and other animals surrounding the pond. Bring a picnic and enjoy a relaxing day or purchase carnival type food through the refreshment stands.

A large pool is open on select spring, summer, and fall days. Paddle boat rentals are also available for $3 (40" tall and up). Also for $3, enjoy a round of mini golf in a course suited for all ages.

Check the website for special events, like Fun Fest with more than 1,000 musical groups competing for prizes.

North / Carrollton
1800 Sandy Lake Road,
Carrollton 75006

972.242.7449

sandylake.com

Admission
Adults: $2
Senior: $2
Children 3 and under:
FREE

Very inexpensive golfing, amusement rides, boat, and train tickets. Pool is $5 for a full day. Miniature golf is $3. Coin operated arcade.

Hours
Mid-March – May:
Saturday & Sunday
10am to 6pm

April & May: Group
Reservations Only

June – Mid-August:
Tuesday – Friday:
10am to 4pm
Saturday & Sunday:
10am to 6pm

Mid-August –
September:
Saturday & Sunday
10am to 6pm

SIX FLAGS HURRICANE HARBOR

Far West / Arlington
1800 E Lamar Blvd,
Arlington 76006

817.640.8900

sixflags.com/
hurricaneharbortexas

Admission
Adults: $32
Children under 48":
$27
Children 2 and under:
FREE

Hours
Varies by season

Hurricane Harbor, a huge water amusement park operated by Six Flags, provides multiple family and kid friendly rides. A favorite for the younger ones is Hook's Lagoon Treehouse with plenty of pirate themed splash opportunities and a lounge areas for parents.

The park includes a lazy river that moves at three miles per hour, multiple slides for older dare devils, and a boogie beach.

Online discount available for single tickets when the purchase is made at least 3 days in advance. Season passes are also available with a pay per month option. Enter online contests for a chance to win free tickets.

SIX FLAGS OVER TEXAS

Far West / Arlington
(Intersection of I-30
and Highway 360)
2201 Road to Six Flags,
Arlington 76010

817.640.8900

sixflags.com/overtexas

Admission
Adults: $65
Children under 48":
$50
Children 2 and under:
FREE

Hours
Varies by season

Who could forget the thrill of their first serious roller coaster ride? Take the heat and lines with stride and enjoy creating some major memories.

Due to the cost and the options for little ones, you may want to hold off on this until your kids are old enough to really take full advantage of all the major rides. That said, once your kids have hit that age (or should I say height restriction), be sure to plan a full day trip.

Online discount available for single tickets when the purchase is made at least 3 days in advance. Season passes are also available with a pay per month option. Enter online contests for a chance to win free tickets.

SKYLINE TRAPEZE

"Unleash your inner circus" at Skyline Trapeze. Classes are offered in flying trapeze, silks, static, Spanish web, juggling, and partner balancing classes.

The two hour flying trapeze classes are recommended for children over 8 years old. Children as young as two can participate in trial swings and special events.

Birthday parties are available for all ages.

Join the mailing list and check the discounted prepaid packages options.

North / Addison
15505 Wright Brothers Drive, Addison 75001

214.771.2406

skylinetrapeze.com

Classes start at $50.

Check schedule and book classes online

SPEED ZONE

Speed Zone offers multiple drag race and go cart tracks, including one called Lil Thunder specially designed for kids under 54" tall. There is also a roller roaster, miniature bowling, miniature golf, and an arcade. Food is from Johnny Rockets.

Starting price is $10 for passengers (includes unlimited rides as a passenger and a round of mini golf) . Starter passes run at $23 (includes four attractions) to $50 for a supercharge pass.

Watch for promo codes and specials throughout the year and consider joining the speed zone club online for special deals.

Speed Zone also offers birthday packages starting at $99.

Northwest
11130 Malibu Drive, Dallas 75229

972.247.7223

speedzone.com

Admission:
Various pass options available.

Hours
Monday - Thursday: 10am to 12am
Friday & Saturday: 10am to 1am
Sunday: 10am to 12am

SURF AND SWIM

**Far Northeast /
Garland**
Audubon Park
440 W. Oates Road,
Garland 75043

972.205.3993

surfandswim.org

Admission
Adults: $8
Children under 48": $6
Children 2 and under:
FREE

Twilight special $2 off
admission after 4pm

Surf in Swim in Garland is a great alternative to the major water parks that provide more activities, but with a higher price tag to match. Save even more by bringing your own cooler (no glass). Try to arrive early to snag a shaded spot to set up for the day.

Large wave pool, splash pad for all ages, cabanas, and snack shop are available at Surf and Swim. Party rentals are also available on select nights.

The park operates from late May through Labor Day. Check the annual calendar online for the current schedule.

TOP GOLF

Northeast
8787 Park Lane
Dallas 75231

214.341.9600

topgolf.com/us/dallas

Hours
Monday - Wednesday:
9am to 12am
Thursday: 9am to 1am
Friday: 9am to 2am
Saturday: 8am to 2am
Sunday: 9am to 12am

The whole family can be entertained at Top Golf which offers pool tables, video games, giant Jenga, and of course...golf! Golf with a twist...each participant hits a golf ball containing a personalized microchip. This microchip computes your score based on the accuracy and distance of the shot and sends the score to a bay screen.

Top Golf also has 54 holes of award winning minature golf (Kids under 12: $6.50 / Adults: $8.75). In addition, batting cages are available and start at $2 for 25 pitches.

TRINITY FOREST AERIAL ADVENTURE PARK

Prepare to challenge yourself, break a sweat, and have some fun. The Trinity Forest Aerial Adventure Park is a combination of canopy tour, military style challenge courses, and zip lines. The six self-guided courses are at three different elevations and four levels of difficulty. Each course becomes higher and gradually more difficult. They each have about 8-12 obstacles.

Participants must be age 6 or older and at least 48" tall and weigh less than 265 lbs.

Birthday party packets are available and start at $300 for 10 participants.

Rates may vary by season. Check online for current pricing and online purchase discounts.

Southeast
1820 Dowdy Ferry Road, Dallas 75217

214.391.1000

rinitytreetops.com

Admission
Adults: $49.95
Senior: $39.95
Children 10 - 15: $44.95
Children 6 – 9: $39.95
Four pack tickets for $135

Hours
Vary by season

WHIRLYBALL AND LASER WHIRLD

Imagine bumper car mixed with lacrosse and maybe a dash of dodgeball and you've got Whirly ball. A truly unique and hilarious experience awaits you in Plano (Hurst location also available). Whirlyball is best played with a large group on a court rented for a couple of hours. For us older adults, expect a bit of a back ache the day after, but the kids can take it.

The facility also has laser tag in a 6,000 sq. ft. two story arena. Up to 25 can play at a time. Don't forget to stop by their arcade. Party packages are available with a starting price of $150 for 10 people.

Hours: Monday - Thursday: 10am to 9pm
Friday: 10am to 12am
Sat.: Noon to 12am / Sun.: Noon to 8pm

Far North / Plano
3115 West Parker Road, Plano 75023

972.398.7900

whirlyballplano.com

Rent a court for 10 or more people:
Half Hour: $75
One Hour: $150
Or pay per person
Half Hour $8
Per Hour $15
1 game (~15 min): $5

Minimum of six are needed to play

193

ZERO GRAVITY THRILL AMUSEMENT PARK DALLAS

Northwest
11131 Malibu Drive,
Dallas 75229

972.484.8359

gojump.com

Admission
One ride: $33
Two rides: $48
Three rides: $50
Five Rides: $78

Hours
Sunday – Thursday:
12pm to 11pm
Friday & Saturday:
12pm to 1am

Thrill seekers this is your place. Zero Gravity offers bungee jumping and five free fall attractions that let you glide 100 feet off the ground.

Party packages are available and start at $28 per person (minimum height is 42"/ minimum participants number is 10).

Check website or call ahead to verify seasonal hours and special late night events.

The Expected to the Unexpected

Are you ready to try something different? Maybe you'd like to escape from a hungry zombie, see a jousting tournament, or stroll through the Ewing ranch. Learn more about these unexpected opportunities in this chapter!

DALLAS PUBLIC LIBRARIES

I almost cried with joy the first time my boys played library at home. Watching them "check out" books at our dining room table was so delightful. Taking my kids to the library is one of my favorite things. My deep love and appreciation for libraries aside.... The Dallas Public Library system is WONDERFUL!

Throughout the city, you can find Children and Teen programs including homework help, poetry and art competitions, reading programs, and guest speaker events. The Dallas Public Libraries also have a great and diverse amount of special events. Check out this small sampling: Fairy Tale Closet (Prom Dress Giveaway); Knitters Anonymous for teens; Youth Leadership – Toastmasters International; Robotics Club; Dinosaur Stomp; Sci-girls Engineer It!; Bridge and Chess Groups; Family Movies; Tales and Tunes for Tots; and Baby Bounce.

Please check the special events calendar and the list of locations available on the web (**dallaslibrary2.org**). The website also provides activity pages and coloring pages all related to the Big D.

Save this number! **214.446.2222**
Dial in any time to hear a prerecorded story provided by Community Partners of Dallas. Call often – new stories are always available.

Downtown: J. Erik Jonsson Central Library
1515 Young Street, Dallas 75201 / 214.670.1700

Even if you live or are staying in another part of town, be sure to plan a trip to one of the largest public library facilities in the nation. Located downtown across from City Hall, the J. Erik Jonsson Central Library has eight floors full or treasures, including Shakespeare's First Folio (1623) and one of the original broadside copies of the Declaration of Independence (printed on July 4, 1776).

The Second floor, the Children's Center, was recently renovated and is a wonderful place with craft tables and magnetic poetry walls.

Teachers! Check out options for the Discovery Wall field trip where children can meet children from around the world in a virtual environment.

LEGOLAND DISCOVERY CENTER

LEGO Factory, 4D Cinema, and 15 rides and attractions make LEGOLAND a full day of fun. For children 4 to 13, the Forest Ranger Pursuit driving adventure will be sure to please. And if you have a little princess, be sure to stop at the Princess Palace and enjoy some karaoke LEGO style. Party packages are available.

Ole Kirk Kristiansen (1851 – 1958) was a carpenter living and running his business in Billund, Denmark. In 1932, he started to build and sell wooden toys. Two years later, he renamed his company LEGO, from the Danish phrase "leg godt", which means play well.

By 1949, LEGO started making the colorful interlocking plastic bricks. In 1958, the LEGO brick we now know was built and patented. Twenty years later, LEGO branched out by adding mini-figures.

The first LEGOLAND Discovery center was opened in Berlin in 2007 with Chicago following in 2008. The Dallas center opened in 2011.

Fun Fact: In 2015, Lego replaced Ferrari as the "World's most powerful brand".

North / Grapevine
Grapevine Mills Mall
3000 Grapevine Mills Parkway,
Grapevine 76051

877.818.1677

legolanddiscovery center.com/dallasfw

Admission
Adults: $21
Children 2 and under: FREE
(Purchase tickets online 24 hours in advance for a discounted rate)

Hours / Holidays
Monday – Friday:
10am to 5pm
Friday & Saturday:
9am to 6:30pm
Sunday:
10am to 4:30pm

MEDIEVAL TIMES DINNER & TOURNAMENT

**Design District /
NE of Downtown**
2021 N. Stemmons,
Dallas 75207

866.543.9637

medievaltimes.com/
dallas.aspx

Admission
Adults: $61
Children 12 and under:
$37
Lap children under 3:
FREE
Ticket packages
available

Witness epic battles of steel and speed while enjoying a utensil-free four course meal "fit for royalty". Take in the live jousting tournament, horsemanship, and falconry.

Join the King's Court for email updates and specials. Also check the website often for special events and sweepstakes.

Free admission on your birthday.

Hours: View show times and make reservations online. Mainly dinner showings, but some educational matinees are provided at lunch.

PALACE OF WAX, RIPLEY'S BELIEVE IT OR NOT! AND ENCHANTED MIRROR MAZE

**Far West /
Grand Prairie**
601 East Palace
Parkway,
Grand Prairie 75050

972.263.2391

ripleys.com/
grandprairie

Admission
Adults: $19
Children 4-12: $9
Children 3 and under:
FREE

Shrunken heads, two headed animals, skulls, unusual artwork and artifacts… It is all waiting for you at Ripley's in the twelve galleries of weird, strange, and the bizarre. Pose for a picture with any of the 200 life-like Hollywood, historic, and the most feared characters in the world. Get lost – really lost – in the 2000 square foot Enchanted Mirror Maze. Get dizzy – really dizzy – in the spinning vortex tunnel. Plan for a two to three hour adventure and leave with big-time memories.

Birthday party packages available; call for additional information.

Hours: Monday - Sunday: 10am to 9pm Seasonal hours may vary.

Reunion Tower is a fifty story iconic tower adjoined to the Hyatt Regency Dallas. The GeO-Deck offers a stunning view of Dallas. Enjoy a closer look through high-definition zoom cameras and telescopes.

Cloud Nine Café is located just above the deck. Fine-dining, Five Sixty by Wolfgang Puck, is located at the top and rotates every evening from 5pm until close. The Kaleidoscope gift shop has unique Big D gifts.

No reservations needed.

Strollers must be left with security and are not allowed up to the GeO-Deck. The deck is ADA compliant and handicap accessible.

Down...
300 Reunion Blvd East,
Dallas 75207

214.712.7040

reuniontower.com

Admission
Adults: $16
Senior: $14
Children 4 - 12: $8
Children 3 and under:
FREE

Combo Day/Night
tickets are available
($13 - $21)

Hours
Monday - Sunday:
10am to 10pm

Last entry
30 minutes prior
to closing

Closed: Christmas

Parking: $6 at the south parking lot at Reunion Boulevard and Sports Streets

DART: Red Line, Blue Line, and Trinity Railway Express stop at Union Station

ROOM ESCAPE ADVENTURES

Far North / Plano
701 Taylor Drive,
Suite 2, Plano 75074

**roomescape
adventures.com**

Tickets: $20-30

Hours
Wednesday - Friday:
6:30 and 8:30
Saturday & Sunday:
12:30pm, 2:30pm,
4:30pm, and 6:30pm

Generally we get in the zombie mood around Halloween, but this venue provides year round terror. The "show" has a maximum of 12 participants who work as a team to escape a room. This interactive production/team building activity allows the group to use wit, problem solving, and communication skills. All of this while a "zombie" is chained to the wall. A buzzer sounds every five minutes and the chain length is extended.

Minimum age to participate without an adult is 14 years. Kids under 14 can participate, but must be accompanied by an adult. It is not recommended for any child under 8 and a waiver must be signed for all participants under 18.

Arrive 15 minutes before show time. Check website or call ahead to verify holiday hours and special late night events.

Private party booking is available.

Fun FAQ from their site:

"Q: Will I really get eaten if I don't escape?

A: Cannibalism has been outlawed since 1804, so the zombie is not legally permitted to eat you."

SOUTHFORK RANCH

Get in the mood by renting the original episodes of *Dallas*, then head to Southfork Ranch to get a taste of the Ewing family life. The guided tour starts with a history of the famous TV Show and the ranch itself. Then enjoy time in the mansion and a stroll through the ranch grounds. There is also a great gift shop with some very spectacular *Dallas* memorabilia that just won't be found elsewhere.

Closes at 3pm on Christmas Eve. Closed on Thanksgiving and Christmas Day.

Check website or call for special late night events.

Far North / Parker
3700 Hogge Road,
Parker 75002

972.442.7800

southforkranch.com

Admission
Adults: $15
Senior: $13
Children 6 - 12: $9
Children 5 and under:
FREE

Hours
Monday - Sunday:
10am to 5pm

ST. MARK'S SCHOOL OF TEXAS PLANETARIUM AND OBSERVATORY

Planetarium Events are open to the public. Check the St. Mark's Events Calendar for options.

**North /
Preston Hollow**
10600 Preston Road,
Dallas 75230

214.346.8000

smtexas.org

Admission: FREE

THANKS-GIVING SQUARE

Downtown
1627 Pacific Avenue,
Dallas 75201

214.969.1977

thanksgiving.org

Admission: Free

Hours
Monday & Tuesday:
Closed
Museum: Wed.-Sat.:
11am to 3pm
Chapel: Wed.-Sun.:
11am to 3pm

DART: Akard Station

Thanks-Giving Square is a three-acre garden, chapel, and museum in downtown Dallas dedicated to giving and living thanks. It celebrated its 50th anniversary in 2014. The garden includes sculptures and water features. The museum includes rare Thanksgiving historical documents.

UNIVERSITY OF NORTH TEXAS (UNT) SKY THEATER

Far Northwest / Denton
University of
North Texas,
1704 W Mulberry
Street, Denton 76201

940.369.8213

skytheater.unt.edu

Admission
$3 and up

Parking: $5, except
on Sundays when it
is FREE

Star Parties are held the first Saturday of every month at the UNT Sky Theater. Learn about the night sky from staff and students and see objects in space through the telescopes available at the Rafes Urban Astronomy Center.

Each month a different show is available at the Children's Matinee which starts at noon ($3 tickets for adults and kids under 12). See Now Showing Schedule on website.

Credit cards are not accepted, bring cash or check.

Historic Districts and Landmarks

Historic preservation efforts in Dallas began in the 70s. Several buildings and neighborhoods have been designated as landmarks, many of which are highlighted in this chapter. For more information, please visit the Dallas Historical Society **dallashistory.org**.

Preservation Dallas
Preservation Dallas champions initiatives to protect the history and culture of neighborhoods and historic buildings throughout the community. Visit the website for information on their fall architectural tours, lecture opportunities, and to download self-guided walking tour brochures for historic neighborhoods.

Preservation Dallas
2922 Swiss Avenue, Dallas 75204
214.821.3573
preservationdallas.org

Universities
There are forty-four colleges and universities in the Metroplex and seven two-year colleges. Some of which have museums or concert venues mentioned in previous chapters. Find the schools closest to you and watch their calendar of events as they usually have great options for guest speakers, volunteer opportunities, and more.

BISHOP ARTS DISTRICT

West Dallas: Bishop Avenue

Very trendy area with galleries, shops, antique stores, and restaurants to suite any taste.

DALLAS ARTS DISTRICT

Downtown

thedallasartsdistrict.org

Dallas has the largest downtown arts and recreation complex in any US city. The transformation started in the 1970s when city officials set their minds on being a world class arts and culture destination. Over the next 40 years, development of the Arts District continued. The Dallas Arts District currently has 68 acres of downtown real estate dedicated to the arts.

Visit www.thedallasartsdistrict.org to schedule an exterior history tour, see special events calendar, or sign up for volunteer opportunities (docents, special events, and internships).

DALLAS CATTLE DRIVE SCULPTURES

Downtown: Dallas Convention Center / Pioneer Plaza, Young St. and S. Griffin St.

Texas size sculptures of longhorns and cowboys. Quick and fun photo op.

DALLAS FARMERS MARKET

Downtown: 1010 S. Pearl Expressway, Dallas 75201

214.664.9110 dallasfarmersmarket.org

South Pearl has been a hub for wholesale farm sales since the late 19th century. By 1941, the site was officially sanctioned as a municipally owned and operated market. The thriving market offers a great variety of food with seasonal variations. Vendor and produce listings are available online. Check hours before you plan your trip.

DEALEY PLAZA

Downtown: 500 Main Street, Dallas 75202

214.571.1000

The site includes the former Texas School Book Depository (see the Arts & Museums chapter) and Dealey Plaza.

DEEP ELLUM

East: Located just East of Downtown

deepellumtexas.com

Deep Ellum started in the late 1800s as a residential and commercial neighborhood for the European immigrant and African-American community. Visit Deep Ellum to see the city's largest collection of preserved storefronts from the early 20th century which now house locally owned shops, restaurants, and galleries. Be sure to stop for a bite at the Twisted Root and Deep Sushi restaurants.

The music scene is also big in Deep Ellum. In the 1920s, the area was a hotbed for blues and early jazz. Today, there are still plenty of music venues and opportunities to take in a show.

Take DART to the Deep Ellum Station and be welcomed by the 38 foot tall Traveling Man sculpture. You will also be able to take in additional great pieces of public art and see the efforts from a community-wide mural project. Check the website for more information on this hip art and music community.

FOUNDERS PLAZA

Downtown: Corner of Market and Elm

Recreation of the mid 1800s log cabin John Neely Bryan built on the Trinity River.

FOUNTAIN PLACE CENTRAL COURT

Downtown: 1445 Ross Ave

fountainplace.com

Visit Fountain Place and see 217 small water jets designed by Dan Kiley, world-class landscape architect. This is a nice place to take a moment of rest and enjoy some peace and quiet while in the bustling Big D.

FREEDMAN'S CEMETERY AND MEMORIAL

Just East of Downtown: Corner of Lemmon Avenue and North Central Expressway, Dallas TX 75223

Freedman's Memorial Cemetery is the resting grounds for more than 5,000 former slaves and the memorial is a homage to those buried there. The 20 foot marble and stone entry arch and bronze sculptures were designed by sculptor David Newton.

David Newton

David Newton is a classically trained sculptor in the European tradition. He was born and raised in Detroit, Michigan. He studied in Detroit, New York, and Florence. His breath taking sculptures at Freedman's Memorial firmly placed him on the national stage.

Look for some of his additional work around Dallas.
- *Texas Woofis in Fair Park*
- *Fair Park Esplanade Fountain in Fair Park*
- *Veterans Memorial in Plano*
- *Exterior Reliefs at the Dallas World Aquarium*
- *Wall Reliefs at Love Field Airport*

J. ERIK JONSSON CENTRAL LIBRARY

Downtown: 1515 Young Street, Dallas 75201

214.670.1700

Even if you live or are staying in another part of town, be sure to plan a trip to one of the largest public library facilities in the nation. Located downtown across from City Hall, the J. Erik Jonsson Central Library has eight floors full or treasures, including Shakespeare's First Folio (1623) and one of the original broadside copies of the Declaration of Independence (printed on July 4, 1776).

The Second floor, the Children's Center, was recently renovated and is a wonderful place with craft tables and magnetic poetry walls.

Teachers! Check out options for the Discovery Wall field trip where children can meet children from around the world in a virtual environment.

JUANITA J. CRAFT CIVIL RIGHTS HOUSE

South Dallas: 2618 Warren Avenue, Dallas 75215

214.670.3687 (City of Dallas Cultural Affairs Office)

nps.gov/nr/travel/civilrights

Juanita J. Craft played a critical role in anti-discrimination efforts in North Texas. She helped organize nearly 100 NAACP chapters and was a leader in the integration efforts for Dallas universities, theaters, restaurants, and the State Fair of Texas.

Lyndon Johnson and Martin Luther King, Jr. visited her modest, single story house to discuss the future of civil rights. Located in the Wheatley Place Historic District just southwest of Downtown Dallas, the house is on the National Park Services list of *Historic Places of the Civil Rights Movement.*

The house is open by appointment. Call the City of Dallas Office of Cultural Affairs office for additional information on visiting and to schedule an appointment.

KENNEDY MEMORIAL PLAZA

Downtown: Main and Market Streets

The Kennedy Memorial Plaza is located a few blocks from Dealey Plaza and the Sixth Floor Museum. It is a simple, but symbolic monument that inspires reflection.

LAS COLINAS/WILLIAMS SQUARE

Far West / Irving: 5221 N. O'Connor Drive, Irving 75039

mustangsoflascolinas.com

When Ben H. Carpenter transformed the land his family ranch was built into a business development, he wanted something to reflect the land's untamed past. In 1976, he commissioned Robert Glen to create the mustangs of Las Colinas. The iconic nine wild mustangs galloping across a granite stream were put in place in 1984.

Adjacent to the sculpture is Williams Square Plaza which includes the Las Colinas Museum.

MUNGER PLACE

NE of Downtown & Deep Ellum: Lying between North Fitzhugh Avenue, Gaston Avenue, Henderson Avenue, and Columbia Avenue

mungerplace.com

In 1905, Robert S. Munger and brother Collett built the "City Man's Home" just minutes from downtown Dallas. The neighborhood was the first deed restricted neighborhood in Dallas. After years of neglect from the Great Depression through the 1960s, restoration on the homes began in the 1970s.

The Munger Place Historic District includes the largest collection of Prairie-Style homes in America (more than 250). Check the website for the tour of homes schedule and Munger Place Days.

REUNION DISTRICT

Downtown: The Reunion District is located in the western portion of downtown and anchored by the Hyatt Regency Dallas and Reunion Tower. Much of the district boarders the Convention Center District.

La Reunion

In 1855, a band of artists, writers, scientists, and musicians established La Reunion outside of Dallas.

The village was inspired by French philosopher Francois Marie Charles Fourier and the goal was to form a socialist Utopian community.

More than three hundred European colonists eventually made La Reunion their home. After the village failed to live up to the dreams of its founders, the area was incorporated into Dallas. Many city landmarks are named after this early settlement.

SWISS AVENUE HISTORIC DISTRICT

NE of Downtown & Deep Ellum: Along Swiss Avenue between La Vista Drive and Fitzhugh Avenue, Dallas 75204

Enjoy a slow stroll or ride through this jaw dropping neighborhood preserved from the early 1900s.

TEXAS LONGHORN CATTLE DRIVE

Downtown: Near Pioneer Plaza / 1428 Young Street, Dallas 75202

The Texas Longhorn Cattle Drive is the biggest outdoor sculpture on earth. Be sure to stop and visit with the fifty running steers herded by three cowboys.

WEST END HISTORIC DISTRICT

Downtown: Includes the west side of Ross Avenue, Elm Street, Main Street, and Jackson Street

dallaswestend.org

The first trading post was opened by John Neely Bryan in what is now known as the West End Historic District. In the late 1800s, the area grew dramatically due to railroad presence. Now, visitors to the West End can enjoy museums, a variety of restaurants, clubs, and shopping.

THE WILSON HOUSE

Just North of Deep Ellum/Wilson Block Historic District: 2922 Swiss Avenue, Dallas 75204

214.821.3573

www.preservationdallas.org

A free tour of the elegant 1899 Queen Anne Victorian mansion, the Wilson House, is provided by Preservation Dallas. No appointment is necessary and the tour is available Tuesday – Friday from 10am to 4pm. Please schedule appointments for group tours.

Are We There Yet? Dallas

Day Tripper

Are We There Yet? Dallas

Fort Worth

"Dallas is where the east ends,
and Fort Worth is notoriously
'where the west begins'."
John Gunther

See what the West has to offer by driving 40 miles west from Dallas or taking the DART TRE line.

AMON CARTER MUSEUM OF AMERICAN ART

3501 Camp Bowie
Boulevard,
Fort Worth 76107

817.738.1933

cartermuseum.org

Admission: FREE!

Hours
Tuesday – Saturday:
10am to 5pm
Sunday: Noon to 5pm

The Amon Carter Museum of American Art is located in Fort Worth's Cultural District. It opened in 1961 due to the generosity of Amon G. Carter Senior.

When you enter the museum, be sure to stop by the Information Desk and ask for a free activity bag. Your children can use it to interact with four different artworks in the collection.

Holidays
Closed: New Year's, Independence Day, Thanksgiving, and Christmas.

CLOUD 9 LIVING

Texas Motor Speedway
3545 Lone Star Circle
Fort Worth 76177

**cloud9living.com/
dallas/stock-car-ride-
along**

Starting at $130

Cloud 9 Living offers a Nascar Ride-Along with 3 or 6 laps around the Texas Motor Speedway. A professional driver steers the 600 horsepower NASCAR stock car around the track while your child enjoys the ride from the passenger seat.

There is no age limit, but riders under 18 must be accompanied by an adult. For safety reasons, the rider must be a minimum height of 5'0 and weigh at least 100 pounds.

Friends and family can come to watch and take pictures.

FOREST PARK RAILROAD

On June 12, 2009, the Forest Park Miniature Railroad celebrated its 50th anniversary. When the five mile Forest Park Miniature Railroad opened in 1959, the large sign at the depot declared it the "longest miniature train in the world". As such, it held the title in the *Guinness Book of World Records*.

Although Forest Park no longer holds this title, you and your family can enjoy the five-mile round trip ride which takes about forty minutes. The train crosses six bridges, including a 350 foot girder and a 175 foot truss bridge, as it makes its way from Forest Park to Duck Pond and back.

1700 Colonial Parkway,
Fort Worth 76101

817.336.3328

fpmt.us

Admission
Adults: $4
Senior: $3.50
Children 13 and under:
$3.50

CASH ONLY!

Check the online calendar for times. Weather can affect routes.

FORT WORTH BOTANIC GARDEN

Enjoy every season at the beautiful Fort Worth Botanic Gardens located just 3.5 miles west of downtown Fort Worth. The 110 acres will provide for a relaxing day with the family as you stroll through the rose, Japanese, and perennial gardens. Enjoy the information boards about the native Texas plants as you view them from the boardwalk.

Bring a picnic and set up near the lovely fragrance garden or grab a bite at the Gardens Restaurant.

Summer camps, the Green Thumb Club, and additional children and family friendly programs are available.

Garden Center, Conservatory, and Japanese Garden hours vary by season.

3220 Botanic Garden
Blvd.,
Fort Worth 76107

817-392-5510

fwbg.org

Admission
Adults: $2 / Senior: $1
Children 4 - 12: $1
Children 4 and under:
FREE!

Hours
Grounds: 365 days
from dusk to dawn

FORT WORTH MUSEUM
OF SCIENCE AND HISTORY

1600 Gendy St.,
Fort Worth 76107

817.255.9300

fwmuseum.org

Admission
Museum and Nobel
Planetarium
Adults: $15
Senior: $13
Children 2 - 12: $11
Children under 2:
FREE

IMAX
Adults: $7
Senior: $6
Children 2 - 12: $6
Children under 2:
FREE

Hours
Monday - Saturday:
10am to 5pm
Sunday: Noon to 5pm

Holidays
Closed: Thanksgiving,
Christmas Eve, and
Christmas

Although the museum has been in existence since 1941, it has seen many changes over the years. The most notable of which took place when it moved to the new facility in 2009. The 166,000 square foot building includes a DinoLab, Dino Dig, the Children's Museum, Energy Blast, and the Cattle Raiser's Museum.

The Children's Museum will definitely provide your kids with an exhilerating, hands-on experience. They can build a train track or play grocery store. They will also get to see live reptiles and amphibians in their natural habitats.

Although the Children's Museum is where your children will want to spend most of their time, the entire museum is very kid-friendly. Your family will probably also want to stay to catch a show at the IMAX dome theater or spend some time at the Noble Planetarium.

216

FORT WORTH NATURE CENTER & REFUGE

Almost 4,000 acres of wilderness comprised of prairies, wetlands, and forest await you at the Fort Worth Nature Center and Refuge.

Enjoy hiking? Pick from over 20 miles of trails or participate in the Nature Hike hosted every Saturday morning.

The Fort Worth Nature Center & Refuge also provides a great variety of educational programs available during the week and on weekends.

Preschool Discovery Club is available for kids 3-5. Pre-registration is required. The cost is $10 per child and covers the admission fee.

Watch for after hours events, such as full moon paddles (age 5 and up), and evening strolls with naturalists.

9601 Fossil Ridge Road, Fort Worth 76135

817.392.7410

fwnaturecenter.org

Admission
Adults: $5
Seniors: $2
Children 3-12: $2
Children 3 and under: FREE!

Hours
Nature Center Refuge:
Weekdays: 7am to 5pm
Weekends: 7am to 7pm

Hardwicke Interpretive Center:
Daily: 9am to 4:40pm

Holidays
Closed: Thanksgiving and Christmas

FORT WORTH STOCKYARDS

East Exchange Ave,
Fort Worth 76176

**fortworth
stockyards.org**

Fort Worth was the last major stop for drovers heading cattle up the Chisholm Trail to the railheads. More than four million head of cattle crossed through Fort Worth, also known as "Cow Town", between 1866 and 1890. As the railway came to Fort Worth, the Union Stockyards were put into full operation around 1889 and became a major shipping point for livestock. By 1902, the Livestock Exchange Building was built and became known as "The Wall Street of the West".

Operations peaked at the Stockyards in 1944. Due to industry changes, outdated plants, and changes in shipping practices, a decline started in the late 1960s and reached an all-time low by 1986. Thankfully, the North Fort Worth Historical Society was chartered and worked to preserve the heritage of the stockyards.

Today, the stockyards are one of Texas' most popular tourist destinations. With the exception of Easter, Thanksgiving, and Christmas, daily cattle drive occurs at 11:30 am and 4pm. The Stockyards Museum, located in the Livestock Exchange Building, is open from 10-5pm (M-Sat and on Sundays June – August / $2 donation per adult appreciated). Spend some time getting lost in the 5,400 square foot Cowtown Cattlepen Maze ($6), shop for a new cowboy hat, or enjoy some steak or bar-b-que at one of the many restaurants in the stockyard station.

FORT WORTH WATER GARDENS

The Fort Worth Water Gardens are often referred to as the "cooling oasis in the concrete jungle". Built in 1974 next to the Fort Worth Convention Center, the 4.3 acre water garden was designed by New York architects John Burgee and Philip Johnson.

There are three pools of water, including a sunken pool that cascades nearly 90 degrees down. Multiple spray fountains, a canopy of large oaks, and water cascades make this a relaxing visit.

South end of down-town between Houston and Commerce Street / Next to the Fort Worth Convention Center

Admission:
FREE!

In 1975, part of *Logan's Run* was filmed in the active pool.

KIMBELL ART MUSEUM

3333 Camp Bowie
Blvd.,
Fort Worth 76107

817.332.8451

kimbellart.org

Admission
Adults: $18
Senior: $16
Children 6 - 11: $14
Children 6 and under:
FREE

Hours
Monday: Closed
Tuesday – Thursday:
10am to 5pm
Friday: Noon to 8pm
Saturday: 10am to 5pm
Sunday: Noon to 5pm

Holidays
Closed: New Year's
Day, July 4th,
Thanksgiving Day, and
Christmas Day

In 1935, Kay and Velma Kimbell bought their first piece of art, "The Artist's Children" by William Beechey. The following year The Kimbell Art Foundation was created by the Kimbells and Kay's sister and brother-in-law. By 1972, eight years after Kay Kimbell passed away and left his fortune to the Foundation, the Kimbell Art Museum opened to the public. By the 40th anniversary in 2012, 10 million people had visited the museum.

Today, the Kimbell collection consists of about 350 works of so-called "definitive excellence" – works that are said to define an artist regardless of the period.

Your children can create their own works of "definitive excellence" at one of the many kid and family programs offered. Plan for a visit during the family festivals, usually with free admission. Check the calendar for the Drop-In Studios dates on select Saturdays (no fee or registration, but space is limited and it is recommended to show up one hour prior to sign up). Summer camps are also available.

THE MODERN

The Modern Art Museum, located in the Fort Worth's Cultural District, is the oldest museum in Texas and one of the oldest museums in the western United States. It was chartered in 1892. The first expedition in 1909 included 45 paintings by contemporary American artists. Now, there are nearly 3,000 post-World War II objects, including paintings, sculptures, videos, photographs, and prints within the 53,000 square feet of gallery space. There is an additional 5,600 square-foot education center and an auditorium.

Free docent-led tours are offered Tuesday through Sunday at 2pm. Consider going on a "Wonderful Wednesday" when a special kid-friendly docent "tour" is provided and your children can participate in story time and an informal drawing exercise related to the works. Admission is free, but attendance is limited.

See the website for additional youth programs offered throughout the year and art camps available for children 4 and up.

3200 Darnell Street,
Fort Worth 76107

817.738.9215

themodern.org

Admission
Adults: $10
Senior: $4
Children 12 and under:
FREE

The Museum is free every Sunday and half price on Wednesday.

Hours
Monday: Closed
Tuesday – Sunday:
10am to 5pm

Holidays
Closed: New Year's Day, Independence Day, Thanksgiving, Christmas Eve, and Christmas

NATIONAL COWGIRL MUSEUM
AND HALL OF FAME

1720 Gendy Street
Fort Worth 76107

817.336.2470

cowgirl.net

Admission
Adults: $10
Seniors & Children
4-12: $8
Children 3 and under:
FREE

Hours
Tuesday - Saturday:
10am to 5pm
Sunday: 12pm to 5pm

The National Cowgirl Museum honors and celebrates women, past and present, whose lives have helped shape the American West. The museum started in 1975 and is currently located in the Fort Worth Cultural District.

You will find interactive exhibit galleries, traveling exhibits, two theaters, a gift shop, and a library.

NATIONAL MULTICULTURAL
WESTERN HERITAGE MUSEUM

3400 Mount Vernon
Avenue
Fort Worth 76105

817.534.8801

cowboysofcolor.org

Admission
Adults: $6
Senior: $4
Students: $3
Children 5 and under:
FREE!

Hours:
Saturday: 12 to 4pm

Founded in 2001, the National Multicultural Western Heritage Museum acknowledges the contributions of individuals of Hispanic, Native American, European, Asian, and African decent to the settlement of the Western American Frontier.

Workshops, history presentations, and a community garden are available. Mark your calendar to attend the free children's storytelling each Saturday from 1 to 3pm.

The museum is also open for groups with appointments on Wednesday through Friday.

Glen Rose

Glen Rose, known as the "Dinosaur Capital of Texas", is about 55 miles southwest of Fort Worth and 75 miles southwest of Dallas. Travel & Leisure Magazine ranked it as one of the "Top 10 Great Weekend Getaways in America".

This small Texas town is home to a little under three thousand residents. The charming downtown square provides local restaurants, specialty shops, historic inns, and the Courthouse built in 1893.

The atmosphere is laid-back and relaxed, but there are great options for activities. The Paluxy and Brazos rivers offer kayaking opportunities and the hill country has plenty of hiking trails and parks. In and around Glen Rose, there are plenty of bed and breakfasts so you can stay and enjoy the small-town charm.

The following pages include some of the best kid-friendly attractions. Also, check out the visitors bureau websites for further information:

www.visitglenrose.com

glenrosetexas.org

DINOSAUR VALLEY STATE PARK

1629 Park Rd 59
Glen Rose 76043

254.897.4588

**tpwd.texas.gov/
state-parks/
dinosaur-valley**

Admission
Adults: $7
Children 12 and under:
FREE

Hours
Daily: 8am to 10pm

Dinosaurs from the cretaceous age left their footprints in the soft shallow sea that covered Texas 113 million years ago. Discovered by nine year old George Adams in 1909, the fossilized tracks of sauropods and theropods can still be seen (and stepped in) in the riverbeds at Dinosaur Valley State Park.

Interpretive center, park store, 20 miles of trails, campsites, swimming, and huge model dinosaurs are available at the park.

DINOSAUR WORLD

Located close to Dinosaur Valley State Park, Dinosaur World provides 20 acres to explore. Along the winding paths and lush gardens there are 150 life size dinosaurs. Regardless of your child's current fascination level with dinosaurs, this adventure will surely spark their interest and imagination.

Let your children take their first stab at being a paleontologist as they uncover a 27 foot skeleton from under sand in the Boneyard or purchase entry to the Fossil Dig ($2) or Dino Gem Excavation ($8 to $13).

Stop at the playground and the prehistoric museum with an impressive collection of claws, eggs, and mammoth bones. Not to ruin the surprise, but if you have little ones be prepared at the end of the museum tour where you will meet motion activated dinosaurs. They will surely provide fright…and delight. As you can imagine, this place has a great gift shop.

10558 Park Road 59,
Glen Rose 76043

254.898.1526

dinosaurworld.com

Admission
Adults: $12.75
Senior: $10.75
Children 3 - 12: $9.75
Children 3 and under:
FREE!

Hours
Monday – Friday:
9am to 5pm
Saturday & Sunday:
9am to 6pm

Holidays
Closed on:
Thanksgiving and
Christmas

FOSSIL RIM WILDLIFE CENTER

2299 County
Road 2008,
Glen Rose 76043

254.897.2960

fossilrim.org

Admission
Adults:
$20.95 weekday
$24.95 weekend

Senior:
$17.95 weekday
$21.25 weekend

Children 3 - 11:
$14.95 weekday
$18.95 weekend

Children 2 and under:
FREE

Feed the animals for $8

Admission
Spring & Summer:
8:30am to 5:30pm
Fall:
8:30 am to 4:30pm
Winter:
8:30am to 3:30pm

Holidays
Closed on:
Thanksgiving Day,
Christmas Eve, and
Christmas Day

Fossil Rim Wildlife Center has over 1000 animals, 50 species of native and non-native animals living peacefully at the 1,700-acre center. Enjoy the afternoon on a Fossil Dig, being a Nature Detective, or participating in the Cheetah Conservation program.

Spend your evening hours in the Discovery After Dark program or consider sleeping over. Lodging is available with rooms starting at $175. The price includes breakfast and scenic wildlife drive pass. For a more economical choice, rustic cabins start at $85 for a party of 5, $10 more per extra guest.

Although the educational programs, including day and overnight camps ($60-$100 with some badge classes) are great, fossil ridge is still best known for the scenic drive. It starts at the Admissions Center where you can purchase snacks for yourself and the animals. You then embark in your own car on the 9.5 mile Scenic Wildlife Drive, observing exotic and endangered species. Savanna-like pastures are home to giraffes, zebras, deer, ostriches, and more.

Are you done with driving by the time you make it to Glen Rose? No problem, take the Guided Tour in open aired safari vehicles. There are many options with various time and price points, so check the website or call before heading there.

Consider purchasing a one or two year membership. Prices vary by party size, but generally are covered within two visits.

Tyler

In just under a two hour road trip heading southeast from Dallas, you can visit Tyler, the "Rose Capital of America". The 22 acre Tyler Municipal Rose Garden is home to 38,000 rose bushes, making it the worlds' largest rose garden.

Although a visit to Tyler will be a great get-away at any time of the year, be sure to check the Rose Season calendar. Each October, thousands of visitors come to Tyler to enjoy the budding roses, garden tours, and community events. The pinnacle event is the Texas Rose Festival, usually held mid-month.

Learn more about Tyler through the Visitors Bureau by visiting: **visittyler.com**

If you are heading to Tyler in June or July, consider altering your route a bit with a stop in nearby Edom, Texas. The treats at the Blueberry Hills Farm are to die for and you can pick your own blueberries or blackberries to snack on while in Tyler.

Blueberry Hills Farm
10268 Farm to Market Road 314
Edom, TX 75756
(903) 852-6175
blueberryhillfarms.com

BROOKSHIRE'S WORLD OF WILDLIFE MUSEUM & COUNTRY STORE

1600 W Southwest Loop 323, Tyler 75701

903.534.3000

brookshires.com/ museum

Admission
FREE

Hours
Tuesday - Saturday
March - September:
9am to 5pm
October - February
9am to 4pm

Wood T. and Louise Brookshire wanted to share their love of wildlife and provide a continuing education experience for children. In 1975, they opened their museum which now receives more than 40,000 visitors per year.

When you stop at Brookshire's you will get to spend some time with the replicas of more than 450 mammals, reptiles, fowl, and aquatic species. Each diorama includes educational information about the animals within.

A shaded picnic area and a playground are available. Your kids will also enjoy the 1950s fire truck, 1936 tractor, and the Country Store filled with products and fixtures commonly seen in the 1920s.

CALDWELL ZOO

2203 Martin Luther King Blvd., Tyler 75702

903.593.0121

caldwellzoo.org

Admission
Adults: $11.50
Seniors: $9.50
Children 3 to 12: $8
Children 2 and under:
FREE

Hours
March 1 - Labor Day:
9am to 5pm
After Labor Day - Feb.:
9am to 4:30pm

Caldwell Zoo is located on 85 acres and has more than three thousand animals. The zoo is dedicated to providing multi-species environments that represent the natural habitats of North America, South America, and East Africa. Your kids will also enjoy the Wild Bird Walkabout, a free-flight aviary with over 600 birds.

Another area they will love is the petting zone with friendly goats and a sand spot with tunnels to climb through.

Camps and classes offered. Closed on New Year's Day, Thanksgiving, and Christmas Day.

CENTER FOR EARTH AND SPACE SCIENCE EDUCATION

The planetarium opened in 1963 at the Tyler Junior College and underwent major renovations in 2011. The facility features exhibits and interactive displays. Dome Shows, including special shows for children, are provided Tuesday through Saturday.

Monthly star parties are free and held monthly. Also watch the calendar of events for promotion kids days when children get in free with an accompanying adult.

Tyler Junior College
1411 E. Lake St.
Tyler 75701

903.510.2312

tjc.edu/cesse

Admission
Adults: $7
Seniors, Students, &
Children: $5

Hours
Tuesday - Friday:
9:30am to 4:30pm
Saturday:
10:30am to 4:30pm

CHEROKEE TRACE DRIVE-THRU SAFARI

Cherokee Trace Drive-Thru Safari, located about 40 minutes south of Tyler, is a wildlife park with over two dozen exotic and endangered species. You and your family can enjoy a self-guided drive in your own vehicle through the hills and open savannas of this 300-acre preserve.

Closed on Easter, Thanksgiving, Christmas Eve, and Christmas Day.

1200 Co Rd 44505
Jacksonville 75766

903.683.3322

cherokeetrace.com

Admission
Adults: $15.95
Seniors: $13.95
Children 3 to 12: $10.95
Children 3 and under:
FREE

Hours
Mon.-Sat.: 10am open
Sunday: 1pm open
Last car admitted:
Between 3:30 to 5:30
depending on season

DISCOVERY SCIENCE PLACE

308 N. Broadway Ave.
Tyler 75702

903.533.8011

**discoveryscience
place.org**

Admission
Adults: $8
Seniors: $6
Children 2 - 12: $5
Children 2 and under:
FREE

Hours
Tuesday - Saturday:
10am to 5pm
Sunday: 1pm to 5pm

Hands-on activities await your children at the Discovery Science Place. A kinetics gallery, Cine Sphere, discovery cave, dino dig, robotics exhibits, and more provide a full day of entertainment and education.

Science Saturdays, held on the first Saturday per month, are great for middle-schoolers and provide presentations and hands-on activities.

Age-appropriate classes, camps, and special events are planned throughout the year.

EAST TEXAS SYMPHONY ORCHESTRA (ETSO)

Administration Offices:
107 E. Erwin
Tyler 75702

903.592.7649

etso.org

The Tyler Symphony Orchestra first performed in 1936. In 1954, it was renamed the East Texas Symphony Orchestra (ETSO). The orchestra performs in venues throughout Tyler and presents it's main series at Liberty Hall in downtown Tyler and the R. Don Cowan Fine and Performing Arts Center located on the University of Texas at Tyler campus.

ETSO has long been committed to education and student performances. Send an email to info@etso.org to join the mailing list for Family Programming.

GOODMAN-LEGRAND MUSEUM AND GARDEN

A historic landmark, the 1859 Goodman-LeGrand House and furnishings were bequeathed to the City of Tyler by the last direct heir to live in the house, Sallie Goodman LeGrand. As per her instructions, the historic family home was opened to the public as a museum. Many of the furnishings, tools, books, and art found within the home date back to the early 1800s.

The grounds of the museum are known as LeGrand Park. Shade trees, azaleas, and roses fill the park that is almost an entire city block. Enjoy a relaxing stroll, bring a picnic, or just relax on the benches provided for visitors.

624 North Broadway
Tyler 75702

903.531.1286

**paksandrec.
cityoftyler.org**

Admission
FREE

Hours
Museum Hours:
Tuesday - Saturday
10am to 4pm
Park & Gardens:
Open Daily
8am to 5pm

TIGER CREEK WILDLIFE REFUGE

Tiger Creek Wildlife Refuge was started in 1998 as a division of the Tiger Missing Link Foundation which documents captive tigers that lived outside of accredited zoos. The sanctuary has led to the rescue of tigers and other species of big cats that were abandoned, neglected, or displaced.

Tiger Creek provides an up-close encounter with lions, leopards, and mountain lions. Your visit will start with a half mile, 30-45 minute guided walking tour. After the tour, guests can walk the facility on their own and enjoy the big cats. Treats & Training and VIP tours are available for an additional fee.

Closed on Sundays and most major holidays.

17552 FM 14
Tyler 75706

903.858.1008

tigercreek.org

Admission
Adults: $15
Seniors: $14
Children 6 to 12: $10
Children 5 and under:
FREE

Hours
Monday -Saturday:
10am to 5pm

Are We There Yet? Dallas

Resources

Important Numbers

- **Emergencies: 911**

- **Texas Poison Center Network: 1.800.222.1222**

Visitors Information

- **Addison**
5300 Belt Line Road
Dallas, TX 75234
addisontexas.net

- **City of Dallas Office of Cultural Affairs (OCA)**
dallasculture.org
The Office of Cultural Affairs works to enhance the vitality of the
City and the quality of life for all Dallas citizens. Through support
and partnership for the 23 city-owned facilities, OCA helps create
environments where art and culture thrive. If you are looking for
something creative and educational, be sure to check the website for
current events.

- **Dallas Convention and Visitors Bureau**
325 North St. Paul Street, Suite 700
Dallas, TX 75201
214.571.1000 / 800.232.5527
visitdallas.com (Spanish: www.visitadallastexas.com)
Free Visitors guide, newsletters, events calendar, and hotel listings
are available online.

- **Farmers Branch**
13000 William Dodson Parkway
Farmers Branch, TX 75234
visitfarmersbranch.com

- **Fort Worth**
111 W. 4th Street, Suite 200
Fort Worth, TX 76102
fortworth.com

- **Frisco**
  6801 Gaylord Parkway,
  Suite 401
  Frisco, TX 75034
  visitfrisco.com
- **Glen Rose**
  1505 NE Big Bend Trail
  Glen Rose, TX 76043
  glenrosetexas.net
- **Grapevine**
  636 S. Main Street
  Grapevine, TX 76051
  grapevinetexasusa.com
- **Mesquite**
  757 N. Galloway Ave
  Mesquite, Texas 75149
  realtexasflavor.com
- **Plano**
  2000 E Spring Creek Pkwy
  Plano, Texas 75074
  visitplano.com
- **Richardson**
  411 West Arapaho Road,
  Suite 105
  Richardson, TX 75080
  richardsontexas.org
- **Tyler**
  PO Box 2039
  Tyler, TX 75710
  cityoftyler.org

Discounts

- **Blue Star Museums**
  arts.gov/national/bluestarmuseums
  Many Dallas Museums participate in the Blue Star Museums
  Program. This national program provides discounts or free
  admission to active-duty military personnel and their families from
  Memorial Day through Labor Day.
- **Dallas City PASS**
  citypass.com/dallas
  Purchase a CityPASS to get admission tickets to four tourist
  attractions in Dallas and save 41% of the regular box office price.
- **Kids Club**
  Kids Club is a partnership between the Crow Collection of Asian Art,
  Dallas Zoo, Perot Museum, Nasher, Trinity River Audubon, and the
  Dallas Museum of Art. You can join the Kids Club at any of these
  organizations.
  Kids Club membership comes with special benefits and discounts
  from all six organizations.

Transportation

- **Dallas Area Rapid Transit (DART)**
  214.979.1111 / dart.org
  DART provides public transportation (buses and trains) in Dallas, Carrollton, Farmers Branch, Garland, Irving, Plano, Richardson, and a Fort Worth and Denton County line.
  DART offers two basic fares:
  $2.50 for all DART buses and trains and TRE service between Union Station and the DFW Airport Station.
  $5 for regional service, which includes all DART buses and trains, all TRE trains plus the T in Fort Worth and DCTA in Denton County.

- **Department of Transportation**
  dfwtraffic.dot.state.tx.us
  Visit website for incidents, lance closures, and rail routes.

- **North Texas Tollway Authority (NTTA)**
  ntta.org
  All tolls in Dallas are cashless. Cars are scanned for a toll tag which deducts the toll from the users' account. If a vehicle does not have a toll tag, a Zip Cash bill will be sent to the owner based on vehicle registration records. The Zip Cash is a 50% premium charge over toll tag pricing. If renting a car, ask the rental agency about the toll tag policy.

Publications

NEWSPAPERS

- **Dallas Morning News**
  508 Young Street, Dallas, TX 75202
  dallnews.com
- **Dallas Observer**
  2501 Oak Lawn Ave., Ste 355, Dallas, TX 75219
  dallasobserver.com
- **Dallas Post Tribune**
  2726 S. Beckley Avenue, Dallas, TX 75224
  dallasposttrib.com
- **Dallas Weekly**
  3101 Martin Luther King Jr Blvd, Dallas TX 75215
  dallasweekly.com
- **Dallas Voice: Premier Media Source for LGBT Texas**
  1825 Market Center Blvd., Suite 240, Dallas, TX 75207
  dallasvoice.com

MAGAZINES

- **Dallas, Fort Worth, and North Texas Child and Baby**
  dfwchild.com
  DFW Child provides the award-winning parenting magazines Dallas
  Child, Fort Worth Child, North Texas Child, Thrive, and Dallas Child
  Baby. Online resources include a great calendar, health and wellness
  tips, travel articles, party suggestions, and special needs information.
- **D Magazine The Dallas Weekly**
  dmagazine.com
  Great food, art, style, wellness, and travel articles.
- **Texas Monthly**
  www.texasmonthly.com
  Politics, food, travel, and culture articles.

Additional Online Resources & Blogs

- **About travel:** gotexas.about.com

- **The Coolest Stuff in Texas:** thecooleststuffintexas.com

- **Dallas Moms Blog:** dallas.citymomsblog.com

- **Dallas Socials:** thedallassocials.com

- **Enkivillage:** enkivillage.com

- **Family Vacation Critic:** familyvacationcritic.com

- **Guide Live:** guidelive.com/things-to-do

- **I Live in Dallas:** iliveindallas.com

- **KERA**
  kera.org / 90.1 FM
  Keep an ear and eye out for the excellent Art and Seek and Kids & Family information provided by KERA, a national public radio affiliate station for North Texas.

- **Metroplex Baby and Kids:** metroplexbaby.com

- **North Texas Kids:** northtexaskids.com
  Entertainment and dining articles, coupons, directories, and an excellent event calendar. Sign-up for eNews is available.

- **Scary Mommy:** scarymommy.com

- **She Knows:** sheknows.com

- **Thrillist:** thrillist.com

- **Tour Texas:** tourtexas.com

- **Travel Savvy Mom:** travelsavvymom.com

Are We There Yet? Dallas

Index

A

Abbott Park 130
Academy of Model Aeronautics (AMA) 29,
    174
Addison Circle Park 130
Addison Octoberfest 43
Addison, TX 40, 41, 43, 50, 64, 114, 130,
    131, 135, 150, 233
Adventure Landing 52, 53, 182
African American Museum 29, 74
Air Travel 4
Alabama-Coushatta Tribe of Texas 11
Albino Alligators 119
Allen, TX 46, 135, 136, 184, 185
Alligators 119
Amazing Jake's Food and Fun 55, 182
American Indian and Southwestern Art
    Market 43
Amon Carter Museum of American Art 29,
    214
Animals 117
Anita N. Martinez Ballet Folklorico 43
Ann and Gabriel Barbier-Mueller Museum
    29, 75
April 37
Aquarium 118, 120, 126, 140
Aquarium Guide 68
Arlington, TX 123, 160, 170, 190
Armadillos 10
Art & Museums 71
August 41
Austin, TX 12, 13
Automobiles 173
Autorama 50
Axolotl 121

B

Babe's Chicken Dinner House 63
Bachman Lake / Bachman Lake Trail 131
Back to School Drive 40, 41
Bahama Beach Waterpark 52, 55, 183
Ballgame 159
Baseball 168, 170
Bath House Cultural Center 29, 76, 114, 157
Beckert Park 40, 41, 131
BEST: Birthday Party 55
BEST: By Age 51
BEST: By Day 33
BEST: By Season 37
BEST: Elementary Age Explorers 52
BEST: Food 61
BEST: Free 29
BEST: Good Deals 31
Best of BIG D 27
BEST: Pre-Teens and Teens 53
BEST: Sleepover 59
BEST: Volunteer Experience 67
Big D NYE 47
Biggest Cowboy 44
Big Orange Pumpkin Farm 43
Big Tex 23, 44, 45
Bioluminescence 40
Birthday 55
Bishop Arts District 204
Black Academy of Arts and Letters 104
Bladderworts 136
Blogs 237
Blueberry Hills Farm 227
Blue Star Museums 73, 234
Bob Jones Nature Center and Preserve 29,
    35, 51, 52, 53, 55, 67, 132
Bob Woodruff Park 133
Bogs 136
Bonnie and Clyde 22
Boo at the Zoo 45

Botanic Garden 127, 137, 215
Bounce House 183, 188
Bounce U 34, 55, 183
Branch Davidians 14
Brookshire's World of Wildlife Museum &
  Country Store 228
Bryan, John Neely 19, 20, 205, 209
Bungee Jumping 194
Butterflies and Bugs! 42
Butterfly Flutterby 43
Butterworts 136

C

Café Silva 65
Café Strada 61
Caldwell Zoo 228
Campion Trails 133
Canton, TX 45
Cara Mia Theater Company 104
Carrollton, TX 63, 139, 189
Cassilly, Bob James 123
Cattle Drive 209, 218
Cattle Drive Sculptures 204
Cedar Hill State Park 31, 52, 53, 134
Cedar Ridge Preserve 29, 35, 67, 134
Celebration Park 135
Celebration Station 33, 34, 184
Celestial Park 135
Center for Earth and Space Science Education
  229
Cherokees 12
Cherokee Trace Drive-Thru Safari 229
Chicken Scratch 62
Children's Aquarium at Fair Park 31, 51, 52,
  55, 59, 118
Children's Chorus of Greater Dallas 105
Children's Health 67
Children's Health Holiday Parade 47
Christmas Boat Parade and Bonfire 47
Christmas in the Branch 47
Chuy's 62
Cinco de Mayo 89

City of Dallas Office of Cultural Affairs (OCA)
  73, 233
City PASS 73
Cloud 9 Living 214
Coat Drive 43
Colony 185
Community Partners of Dallas 37, 40, 41,
  43, 46, 47, 50, 67
Connemara Meadow Preserve 42, 136
Conservation Guide 68
Cosmic Jump 55, 184
Cotton Bowl 49
Cotton Bowl Parade of Bands 47
Cottonwood Arts Festival 38, 43
Cowboys Trivia 161
Cowgirl 222
Cow Town 218
Craft, Juanita J. 207
Creative Arts Center of Dallas 53
Crossroads Diner 65
Crow Collection After Dark 42, 50
Crow Collection of Asian Art 77
Crow Museum of Art 29, 34, 35, 40, 42, 50,
  51, 73
Crybaby Matinee 33, 51, 105

D

Dallas Angelika Film Center 33, 51, 105
Dallas Arboretum and Botanical Gardens 34,
  41, 42, 43, 47, 52, 53, 137
Dallas Area Kitefliers Organization (DAKO)
  29, 174
Dallas Area Rapid Transit (DART) 235
Dallas Arts District 25, 67, 72, 204
Dallas Black Dance Theatre 106
Dallas Cattle Drive Sculptures 204
Dallas Children's Medical Center 25
Dallas Children's Theater 51, 52, 67, 106
Dallas City PASS 73, 234
Dallas City Slogan 19
Dallas Contemporary 29, 78
Dallas Convention and Visitors Bureau 233
Dallas Convention Center 204

Dallas Cowboys 24, 160

Dallas Dance Festival 46

Dallas Desperados 162

Dallas Exposition 22

Dallas Farmers Market 204

Dallas Firefighter's Museum 45, 52, 175

Dallas/Fort Worth International Airport (DFW) 15

Dallas Heritage Village 29, 31, 33, 36, 46, 47, 51, 53, 55, 67, 79

Dallas Historical Society 203

Dallas Holocaust Museum 53, 67, 80

Dallas International Guitar Festival 53

Dallas Mavericks Basketball 29, 163

Dallas Morning News 236

Dallas Museum of Art 29, 33, 34, 51, 52, 53, 73, 81

Dallas Name Origin 19

Dallas Nickname 19

Dallas Observer 236

Dallas Opera 52, 53

Dallas Parks and Recreation 67, 159

Dallas Polo Club 164

Dallas Population 18

Dallas Post Tribune 236

Dallas Pride Parade 42

Dallas Public Libraries 29, 51, 52, 53, 68, 196

Dallas Puppet Theater 107

Dallas Stars Hockey Club 29, 165

Dallas Summer Musicals 29, 41, 108

Dallas Symphony Orchestra 29, 45, 49, 52, 53, 109

Dallas Theatre Center 42

Dallas Timeline 21

Dallas Voice 236

Dallas Weekly 236

Dallas Winds 110

Dallas World Aquarium 51, 52, 120

Dallas Zoo 22, 31, 33, 34, 35, 45, 49, 50, 51, 52, 55, 59, 68, 73, 122, 176

DART 235

Day Tripper 211

Dealey Plaza 68, 98, 205, 207

December 47

Declaration of Independence 206

Deep Ellum 205

Deep Sushi 205

Denton Arthur Coley 103

Department of Transportation 235

Devil's Bowl Speedway 35, 50, 166

DFW Airport 176

Dickens of a Christmas 47

Dinosaur 95, 196, 223, 224, 225

Dinosaur Capital of Texas 223

Dinosaur Valley State Park 224

Dinosaur World 225

Dirt Track Races 166

Discounts 73, 234

Discovery Science Place 230

D Magazine 236

Dough Pizzeria Napoletana 62

Dragon Park 52, 138

Dream Café 63, 64

Drive-In 111

Dr Pepper 15

Dr. Pepper Star Centers 55

DSM Kids Club 29

Duck Creek Greenbelt 138

E

Earth Day Texas 38

Easter Basket Drive 50

EAST Texas Symphony Orchestra (ETSO) 230

Eisenhower, Dwight D. 16

Ellen's Southern Kitchen 61

Elm Fork Nature Preserve 139

Emergencies: 911 233

Emergency Medical Kit 5

Euless, TX 37, 165

Ewing, J.R. 25

Expected to the Unexpected 195

F

Fair Park 19, 21, 22, 31, 41, 45, 49, 52, 53, 74, 97, 100, 114, 118, 122, 127, 140, 175, 180, 206

Fall 43

Fall Equinox 43

Famous Texans 17

Fangs! 40

Farmers Branch, TX 38, 41, 42, 45, 46, 47, 141, 165, 186, 233, 235

Farmers Market 204

Farmstead Museum 52

FC Dallas Soccer Club (MLS) 29, 31, 167

February 50

Ferguson, Ben 71

Ferguson, Jim and Miriam Amanda Wallace 16

Film 103

Film, Theater, and the Sound of Music 103

Fine Arts Chamber Players 29, 52, 53, 110

Fireflies 40

Flower Mound Pumpkin Patch 45

Flower Mound, TX 45, 186

Forest Park Miniature Railroad 31

Forest Park Railroad 215

Forney, TX 38, 45, 55, 124

Fort Paintball 53, 185

Fort Worth Botanic Gardens 31, 215

Fort Worth Museum of Science and History 216

Fort Worth Nature Center & Refuge 217

Fort Worth Stockyards 218

Fort Worth, TX 30, 31, 33, 36, 38, 213, 233

Fort Worth Water Gardens 219

Fossil Rim Wildlife Center 59, 68, 226

Founder's Plaza Plane Observation Area 176, 205

Fountain Place Central Court 205

FREE 29

Freedman's Cemetery and Memorial 206

Friday 34

Friends of the Lake 70

Frisco Fire Safety Town 29, 41, 45, 47, 52, 68, 177

Frisco Rough Riders 30, 57, 168

Frisco, TX 25, 29, 30, 38, 41, 45, 47, 52, 57, 68, 101, 165, 167, 168, 177, 180, 187, 188, 234

Frog Club 123

Froggie's 5 & 10 63

Frontiers of Flight 31, 41, 51, 52, 53, 55, 178

Ft. Worth Stockyards 179

Fun Fest 189

G

Galaxy Drive-In 52, 53, 111

Galveston 13

Gardeners in Community Development 68

Garland, TX 31, 51, 63, 138, 192, 235

Gaylord Texan Resort & Convention Center 47

Gentle Zoo 55, 124

Geometric MADI Museum 30, 82

German Chocolate Cake 25

Glen Rose, TX 223, 234

Go Carts 188, 191

Good Deals 31

Goodman-Legrand Museum and Garden 231

Goss-Michael Foundation 30, 35, 83

Grand Prairie Airhogs 168

Grand Prairie, TX 45, 52, 54, 56, 142, 168, 169, 198

GrapeFest 42

Grapevine Springs Preserve 142

Grapevine, TX 38, 42, 43, 45, 47, 51, 52, 54, 126, 132, 142, 179, 197, 234

Grapevine Vintage Railroad 35, 45, 47, 51, 52, 179

Great Trinity Forest 148

Greek Food Festival of Dallas 42

Green Thumb Club 215

Greenville Avenue St. Patrick's Day Parade 50

Guinness Book of World Records 215

Gunter, TX 43

Gunther, John 213

H

Habitat for Humanity 68
Habitat Restoration Day 70
Halloween in the Park 45
Halloween Organ Spooktacular 45
Halloween Scream Train 45
Hawaiian Falls Adventure Park 52, 53, 55,
    185
Heard Natural Science Museum and Wildlife
    Sanctuary 35, 52, 53, 55, 125
Heart Beats 103
Heisman 17
Heritage Farmstead Museum 31, 34, 51, 52,
    53, 84
Heritage Village 41
Highland Park 47
Highland Park Old Fashioned Soda Fountain
    63
Hispanic Expo 42
Historic Districts and Landmarks 203
Historic Places of the Civil Rights Movement
    207
History of Dallas 20
Hockey 165
Holiday Toy Drive 46, 47
Horse Colleges 175
Horse Races 169
Houston, Sam 12, 16
Hunger Action Month 42
Hunt, Lamar 23
Hurricane Rita 14

I

ICE! 47
IMAX 216
Independence Day 41
Independence from Mexico 12
Indoor Safari Park 55, 186
International Museum of Cultures 30, 42, 86
Into the Meadow 42
Irving Arts Center 34, 51, 52, 87

Irving, TX 34, 87, 92, 133, 162, 165, 176,
    207, 235

J

January 49
J. Erik Jonsson Central Library 196, 206
Joe Pool Lake 134, 142
Johnson, Lyndon B. 14, 16
Johnson Space Center 14
Jones, John Dolford "Bob" 132
Joppa Preserve 143
Jordan, Barbara 14
Juanita J. Craft Civil Rights House 207
July 41
June 40
Juneteenth Celebrations 40
Junior Camp Counselor 68
Junior Historians 67
Junior Zookeeper 68

K

Kaboom Town 41
Kathy Burks Theatre of Puppetry Arts 111
Katy Trail 143
Keller's Drive-In 64
Kennedy Memorial Plaza 207
Kennedy, President John F. 14, 16, 21, 23,
    98, 99, 207
KERA 73, 237
Kickapoo Traditional Tribe of Texas 11
Kidd Springs Park 144
Kid Film Festival 49
Kids Club 73, 234
Kiest Park 52, 53, 144
Kilby, Jack 23
Kilgore, TX 22
Kimbell Art Museum 220
Kirin Court 64
Kites 174
Klyde Warren Park 30, 33, 51, 52, 53, 145
Kristiansen, Ole Kirk 197

L

Lake Cliff Park 52, 53, 146
Lakeside Park 51, 52, 53, 146
Landmarks 203
La Reunion 208
Las Colinas 207
Laser Tag 182, 193
Latino Cultural Center 30, 35, 51, 52, 53, 68, 88
LEGO 197
LEGOland Discovery Center 197
Lemons to Aid 68
Lewisville Lake Environmental Learning Area 34, 35, 68, 147
Liberty Park 51, 52, 147
Lil Ninjas 55, 186
Little Rookies 29
Livestock Exchange Building 218
Local Explorers 4
Lockhart Smokehouse BBQ 62, 64
Logan's Run 219
Lone Star Park 169
Love Field 178
Lunar Mini Golf 55, 187
Lynn Creek Park 47

M

MADI Manifesto 82
Magazines 236
Magic Time Machine 64
Main Event 53, 55, 187
Main Street Garden Park 148
Majestic Theatre 47, 112
Marcus, Herbert 24
Margarita 24
Martinez, Mariano 24
Martin Luther King Jr Parade 49
McKinney Avenue Transit Authority 30, 56
McKinney Avenue Trolley (M-Line) 180
McKinney, TX 30, 45, 47, 56, 125, 165
Meadows Museum of Art 30, 34, 36, 53, 90
Meadows School of the Arts 113
Meals on Wheels 70
Medieval Times Dinner & Tournament 57, 198
Meetup/Random Acts of Kindness 68
Mesquite Championship Rodeo 40, 52, 53, 169
Mesquite, TX 38, 40, 52, 53, 166, 169, 184, 234
Metropolitan Winds 30, 112
Mexican Independence Day 89
Mexican War 12
Meyerson Symphony Center 72
Mideival Times Dinner & Tournament 30
Mini Golf 31, 111, 182, 184, 186, 187, 189, 191, 192
M-Line 30, 180
MLK Day of Service 49
MLS 167
Modern 221
Monarch Butterfly 10
Monday 33
Monorail Safari 176
Moon Day 41
Moore Park 148
Morton H. Meyerson Symphony Center 113
Munger Place 208
Munger Place Historic District 208
Municipal Rose Garden 227
Museum of the American Railroad 180
Music 103
Music Hall at Fair Park 114
Myerson Symphony Center 47
My Favorite Day 33

N

Nasher Sculpture Center 30, 35, 50, 51, 52, 53, 72, 73, 91
National Aeronautics and Space Administration (NASA) 14
National Cowgirl Museum and Hall of Fame 222
National Fire Prevention Week 45
National Fishing Week 40

National Model Aviation Museum 174
National Multicultural Western Heritage
    Museum 222
National Public Radio 73
National Scouting Museum 30, 33, 36, 52,
    92
Native American Reservations 11
Nature Center 132, 217
Nature Preserve 125, 132, 134, 136, 139,
    142, 143, 149, 152, 229
NBA 163
Newspapers 236
Newton, David 206
New Year's Eve 47
NFL 160
NHL 165
Nip and Tuck's Barnyard Buddy Stories 51
North Park Center 47
North Pole Express 47
North Texas Food Bank 42, 68
North Texas Irish Festival 50
North Texas Tollway Authority (NTTA) 235
November 46
Nutcracker 47

O

Oak Cliff 24, 30, 93, 104, 122, 144, 146
Oak Cliff Cultural Center 30, 93
Oak Point Park & Nature Preserve 149
October 43
Oil Boom 13
Old Red Museum 31, 36, 52, 94
Online Resources 237
Opera 29, 31, 52, 53, 107, 114
Orchestra 29, 38, 45, 49, 52, 53, 105, 109,
    113, 230
Oswald, Lee Harvey 23
Out of the Loop Fringe Festival 50
Owl-O-Ween 45

P

Paddle Boat 189
Paedomorphism 121

Paintball 185
Palace of Wax, Ripley's Believe It or Not! 198
Parks 129
Perot Museum 33, 34, 35, 51, 52, 54, 56,
    59, 73, 95, 97
Pet Parade 45
Pitfall Traps 136
Plane Observation Area 176
Planes 173
Planetarium 30, 96, 201, 216, 229
Plano Balloon Festival 42
Plano Trails 149
Plano, TX 31, 34, 42, 57, 64, 84, 133, 147,
    149, 165, 182, 183, 187, 193, 200, 234,
    235
Pleasant Oaks Park 51, 52, 150
Pocket Sandwich Theatre 34, 54, 115
Poison Center Network 233
Pole Position Raceway 56, 188
Polo 164
PreK and Under 51
Preservation Dallas 30, 203
Pritzker Architecture Prize 72
Publications 236
Pump It Up 56, 188
Pumpkins on the Prairie 45
Puppets 111

Q

Quorum Park 150

R

Random Acts of Kindness 68
Random Dallas Facts 24
Random Texas Facts 15
Renaissance Festival 38
Republic of Mexico 12
Resources 233
Reunion District 208
Reunion Tower 199
Reverchon Park 151
Richardson, TX 38, 43, 115, 165, 234, 235
Ripley's Believe It or Not! 45, 52, 54, 56

Robert E. Lee Park 152
Rodeo 17, 40, 46, 52, 53, 169
Rookie Camps 171
Room Escape Adventures 54, 56, 200
Roosevelt, Theodore 22
Rowlett Creek Nature Preserve Trails 152
Rowlett, TX 152
Ruby, Jack 23
Russian Festival 50

S

Samurai Collection 75
San Antonio, TX 12
Sandy Lake Amusement Park 31, 40, 51, 52, 189
Saturday 35
Scarborough Renaissance Festival 38
Sea Life Grapevine Aquarium 51, 52, 54, 56, 126
Shakespeare Dallas 114
Six Flags Hurricane Harbor 52, 54, 190
Six Flags Over Texas 45, 52, 54, 190
Sixth Floor Museum 54, 68, 98, 207
Skyline Trapeze 54, 56, 191
Sky Theater 202
Slaughter, TX 15
Sleepover 59
Soccer 167
SoupMobile 69
South Dallas Cultural Center 30, 100
Southfork Ranch 201
Southlake, TX 51, 53, 67, 132
Southpaw's Organic Grill 63
Space Shuttle Columbia 14
Speed Zone 52, 54, 56, 191
Spirit of Texas 178
Spring 37
Spring Equinox 37
Star Center Rinks 165
Start 62, 65
State Fair of Texas 22, 23, 43, 44, 45, 118, 140, 207
State Insects and Animals 10

State Motto 9
State Plants, Vegetables, and Food 10
State Song 9
St. Mark's School of Texas Planetarium and Observatory 30, 201
Stockyards 218
Stockyards Museum 218
Strauss, Annette 23
Studio Bella 69
Summer 41
Summer Solstice 41
Sunday 36
Sundews 136
Surf and Swim 31, 51, 192
Susan G. Komen Breast Cancer Foundation, Inc. 69
Swiss Avenue Historic District 209
Symphony 29, 45, 47, 49, 52, 53, 72, 113, 230

T

Take Me Out to the Ballgame 159
Taste of Dallas 41
TeenLife 69
Texas Ballet 30, 47, 115
Texas Black Invitational Rodeo 40
Texas Centennial Exposition 22
Texas Discovery Gardens 30, 31, 33, 40, 42, 45, 51, 52, 57, 127
Texas Flag 9
Texas Home & Garden Show 42, 49
Texas Longhorn Cattle Drive 209
Texas Monthly 236
Texas Rangers 31, 170
Texas Rangers Youth Ballpark 57
Texas Red Nations Powwow 46
Texas School Book Depository 99, 205
Texas Scottish Rite Hospital 69
Texas Sculpture Garden 30, 101
Texas Stampede Rodeo 46
Texas Statehood 12
Texas Timeline 11
Thanks-Giving Square 202

Theatre 103
The Dallas Opera 29, 31, 107
The Gentle Zoo 45, 51
The Modern 30, 33, 36
The Perot Museum Fair Park Campus 31
The Wilson House Tour 30
Thursday 34
Tiger Creek Wildlife Refuge 231
Tiger Missing Link Foundation 231
Tollway 235
Top Golf 52, 54, 192
Toyota Stadium and Toyota Soccer Center 167
Traditional Fun Zones 181
Trains 25, 31, 35, 38, 45, 47, 55, 124, 173, 176, 179, 186, 189, 215, 216, 235
Trains, Planes, and Automobiles 173
Trampoline 184
Trapeze 191
Travel Bag 4
Traveling Man sculpture 205
Traveling with Children 3
Trinity Forest Aerial Adventure Park 54, 57, 193
Trinity Forest and River 153
Trinity River Audubon 30, 31, 34, 35, 36, 40, 42, 45, 51, 52, 54, 57, 70, 73, 154
Trinity River Expeditions 35, 52, 54, 156
Truck Yard 65
Tucker Hill Pumpkinville 45
Tuesday 33
Turtle Creek Greenbelt 156
Twinkle Light Boat Parade 47
Twisted Root 205
Tyler Municipal Rose Garden 17, 227
Tyler, TX 37, 227, 234

U

Union 13
United Way 70
Universities 203
University of Dallas 23
University of Texas 13

UNT Sky Theater 35, 36, 51, 52, 202

V

Venus flytrap 136
Veterans Day Celebration 46
Victory Park 47
Viva Dallas! 42
Viva Dallas! Hispanic Expo 42
VNA Meals on Wheels 70
Volunteer Match 70
Volunteer Now 70

W

Waterpark 181, 183, 185, 190, 192
Wednesday 33
Wee Volunteer 70
West End Historic District 209
West Nile Virus 14, 39
Whirlyball and Laser Whirld 57, 193
White Rock Creek Trail 157
White Rock Lake 35, 51, 52, 54, 65, 70, 76, 131, 137, 157
Wild About Harry's 63
Williams Square 207
Wilson Block Historic District 209
Wilson House 209
Winspear Opera House 72
Winter 49
Winter Solstice 49
Women's Right to Vote 13
Wyly Theatre 72

Y

Yester Land Farm 45
Yoginos 35, 51
Yolk One Arts Plaza 61
Young Dragons 51
Ysleta del Sur Pueblo 11

Z

Zero Gravity 54, 57, 194
Zoo 122, 124, 176, 228